THE McGRAW-HILL

Working Drawing
Planning
and
Management
Manual

THE McGRAW-HILL

Working Drawing Planning and Management Manual

Fred A. Stitt

McGRAW-HILL BOOK COMPANY

New York St. Louis San Francisco Auckland Bogotá
Hamburg Johannesburg London Madrid Mexico
Montreal New Delhi Panama Paris São Paulo
Singapore Sydney Tokyo Toronto

Library of Congress Cataloging in Publication Data

Stitt, Fred A.

   The McGraw-Hill working drawing planning and
management manual.

   1. Building — Details — Drawings. I. Title.
TH431.S75   1985   692'.2   85-9848
   ISBN 0-07-061553-5 (pbk.)

1234567890   SEM/SEM   898765

ISBN 0-07-061553-5

The editors for this book were Joan Zseleczky and Barbara B. Toniolo
and the production supervisor was Thomas G. Kowalczyk.

Printed and bound by Semline, Inc.

CONTENTS

PREFACE

Every year 30 to 40 percent of insured design firms are sued. Many lawsuits are unjustified, but many others are 100 percent valid and due mainly to lapses in working drawings and specifications.

Even a trivial working drawing oversight discovered during construction can cost a design firm several hundred dollars just for processing the change order.

When the contractor finds major omissions, or when drawings include contradictions or conflicts, the added costs rise from hundreds of dollars to many thousands.

Here's how this checklist manual attacks such problems:

1. It's a reminder and drawing planning guide for the project manager, listing virtually all items that are normally included on every type of architectural working drawing sheet.

2. Once the project manager marks job-related items, sections of the list become instruction guides to drafters to show them what goes on the drawings.

3. It's a checklist on which drafters mark what they complete as they complete it, and a place for them to write questions.

4. It's a checking guide for each checkprint review.

5. As a list is checked off, it becomes a checklist of items that also must be in specifications. This specifications checklist is created automatically during the planning and checking processes. Every building component listed includes its CSI correlated specification division number for easy cross-reference.

6. As the list is used on a job, it becomes an automatic checklist of items to be detailed. The CSI coordination numbers with each item also serve as file numbers for locating relevant details in your standard detail library or on computer.

7. It's a guide for coordinating varied types of drawings and for cross-checking drawings from different consultants.

8. It's a guide to related information that must be included with each building component, such as generic materials identification; dimensions, locations, spacings, and heights; detail keys; and notes and references.

In total, this is one of the most useful tools one can have for planning, supervising, checking, and coordinating construction documents. It's designed for offices and projects of all sizes and applies equally to hand drafting, Systems Drafting, and CADD. The manual also includes numerous special tips for doing production drawings most efficiently.

About the Author

Fred A. Stitt is an architect, writer, editor, publisher, and inventor with extensive experience in design and problem solving. Since 1969 Stitt has produced Guidelines Publications on architectural planning, creative problem solving, materials failures, A/E computerization, and many other subjects for architects and engineers. He is the author of the widely acclaimed McGraw-Hill books *Systems Drafting* (1980) and *Systems Graphics* (1983) and currently has several other books in preparation. In addition to writing and publishing *The Guidelines Letter*, the first successful newsletter on design firm management, Mr. Stitt also writes articles for publications such as *Repro Graphics World, Architectural Record,* and *Design Book Review.*

This author lectures widely in the United States and overseas for professional societies and universities. His own Guidelines workshops and conferences on reprographic systems, computers, design management, and the future of architecture have been attended by nearly 10,000 design professionals.

He is currently establishing a private architectural school and research institute on architectural education in the San Francisco Bay Area under the auspices of a nonprofit corporation, The GL Foundation.

INSTRUCTIONS FOR USING THE CHECKLIST SYSTEM

THE CHECKLIST ENTRY FORMAT

Here's a typical checklist segment and a description of what each item means:

```
       IN    OK

1)    ___   ___    FLOOR DRAINS  15400  (15421)
2)                 ___ slope floors to drain
3)                 ___ locations ___ detail keys ___ notes/refs
4)                 coord check: ___ struct ___ hvac
```

Item 1)   Identifies the generic component with its broadscope CSI Masterformat specification number shown first. The number in parentheses is a narrowscope number that also identifies the component's standard detail file number.

A construction component checked as "IN" must be included in broadscope working drawings. Each one checked as "IN" will most likely also have to be detailed and/or included in specifications.

Item 2)   A reminder note regarding related requirements.

Item 3)   Usually consists of reminders to show or note the following:
___ Materials (not relevant in this example).
___ Sizes, heights, locations, or object dimensions as appropriate.
___ Detail keys if required.
___ Identification note and, sometimes, reference to other drawings or documents.

At the close of a job, a final check in the "OK" slot means that all these items and Item 4 have been checked and are satisfactory.

Item 4)   The "Coordination Check" refers both drafter and checker to other construction components that may relate to this one, to other drawings that may reference the same component, and to other parts of the documents that may need to be checked to search for conflicts or interferences. In this example, since drains are sometimes positioned badly relative to under-floor structural or mechanical work, this "coord check:" note provides a reminder to look for possible interferences.

INSTRUCTIONS FOR USING THE CHECKLIST SYSTEM Continued

    Using this checklist system is very similar to using outline speci-
fications. You can use the list any number of ways, for example:

____ You can distribute copies of appropriate sections of the checklist
to drafting staff and have them mark off items they include in
the drawings in the "IN" slots. Later you can check the items
as being complete and correct in the "OK" slot. All items not
"OK" remain clearly visible on the list until they're completed.

OR

____ You, or a drafting supervisor, can plan the work of the drafters
by marking up copies of the checklist sections in these steps:

    ___ Cross out items clearly not to be included in the drawings.

    ___ Mark questionable items in pencil with a "?" in the IN slot.

    ___ Put a checkmark in the "IN" slot for items that will be in
the working drawings.

    ___ Have the drafters cross out the checkmarks in the "IN" slots
when they complete the item. Later, add checkmarks in the
"OK" slots to show that items have been checked and are completed as required. If they're not yet complete, add a
circle in the "OK" slot to show it still needs to be done.

    ___ For most thorough checking do a final quality control check
before submittal for bids. Add final dual checkmarks in the
"OK" slots to confirm that everything is complete and correct.

    Before using the list on a project, make a photocopy of the orig-
inal. Save the original to copy again for other projects. Your right
to copy is specifically limited to your own use, of course.

    THE WORK ON ANY DRAWING MAY BE RELEVANT TO OTHER DRAWINGS OR BE
AFFECTED IN TURN BY OTHER ARCHITECTURAL OR CONSULTANTS' WORK. KEYS TO
THESE ARE CITED AS "COORD CHECK" (COORDINATION CHECK) NOTES IN THE LIST.
THIS IS ONE OF THE MOST IMPORTANT ASPECTS OF THE CHECKLIST.

    When checking the documents, follow your normal checkprint marking
process. (Presumably, you'll mark ok items with yellow, additions in
green, corrections and changes in red--standard practice.)

    BE SURE TO USE THE "OK" COLUMN FOR THE FINAL PHASE OF CHECKING
AND DRAWING REVIEW.

INSTRUCTIONS FOR USING THE CHECKLIST SYSTEM   Continued

Return newly marked copies of checkprints and checklists to drafting staff for finish-up work. Date and keep the old copies, and date the new ones.

As the list develops simultaneously with the working drawings, you'll have a checklist of specifiable items complete with their CSI Masterformat identification numbers. Updated copies of the list can go to the spec writer as specifications/working drawing coordination memos. (We recommend and are using Masterformat MP-2-1. The later Masterformat version MP-2-3 is not satisfactory for thorough detail and specification coordination. However, if you must use MP-2-3, or any other specification numbering system, just modify the specification numbers on your original.)

As the drawings and the list develop through various checking phases, you'll have a checklist of the details to be included. Flag the detail items as a guide for your detail drafting staff. If you have a standard detail library such as the one produced by GUIDELINES, you'll have the CSI-coordinated index numbers necessary to retrieve the details from your files.

Give special attention to the introductory notes in each chapter on what to avoid on the drawings, on coordination among different drawings, and on the best applications of systems drafting. If you review these early in the game, you and your staff will gain many multiple values from using the checklist.

LEXICON OF ABBREVIATIONS

Most abbreviations are self-evident, such as "fl plan" for "Floor Plan" but "anch" or "sup" might not be immediately clear.

Here's a list of abbreviations used in different parts of this list, mainly in the Coordination Check notes.

acoust   Acoustical treatment drawings.

anch   Anchor. The most common oversight in working drawings and
            construction is related to anchors and connectors between
            various components. The importance of checking these is em-
            phasized throughout and given special note in terms of "fl
            anch" for floor anchor, "clg anch" for ceiling anchor, etc.

civil/soil Civil engineering drawings as for grading and drainage.

code   Building code, fire code or other applicable regulations.

INSTRUCTIONS FOR USING THE CHECKLIST SYSTEM Continued

const site	Construction work site plans.
cross sect	Cross sections.
drain	Drainage. Most often a part of site plans.
elec	Electrical.
ext elev	Exterior elevations.
fin sched	Finish schedules.
fl plan	Floor plans.
frame	Framing, either structural or non-structural wall framing.
furn	Furniture.
hardwr	Hardware.
hvac	Heating, Ventilating, and Air Conditioning.
int elev	Interior elevations.
landsc	Landscaping
mech	Encompasses both hvac and plumbing.
pl	Plan.
plumb	Plumbing.
ref clg	Reflected Ceiling.
sched	Schedules.
sect	Sections.
site	Sitework.
specs	Specifications.
struct	Structural.
sup	Support. Implying anchorage of an item of construction with curbs, pedestals, or added structural support.
util	Utility such as water/gas/sewer/steam/communcations/power.
vent	Ventilation. Part of hvac or mech--air distribution.

INSTRUCTIONS FOR USING THE CHECKLIST SYSTEM   Continued

HOW TO ADD DOCUMENTATION OF JOB CHANGES

Conflicts often arise during and after a project as to the causes of extra work and costs. Memories fade and honest misunderstandings are common. You can use the method described below to augment your job records regarding day-to-day decisions and changes.

As changes are noted, jot down the dates and a coded reason and source for each change on the appropriate item (or on the back of the sheet and add a flag on the front). Even a shorthand record will go a long way toward clarifying the job's history and sequence of decision making.

A suggested code for noting reasons for decisions are:

BC   By client. Changes initiated for whatever reasons of preference. These items are the most important to record and date because they are most likely to affect both the Scope of Work by the architect and the construction budget. The effects of changes should be studied and reviewed with the client to assure there is full mutual understanding of the financial implications of any change both in document production and construction.

CR   Code requirement or just a general safety consideration whether required by law or not. (Note code sources and section numbers.)

DC   Design/aesthetics consideration. Architect initiated unless noted otherwise.

EC   Economics.

CC   Change necessitated to coordinate work properly with consultants.

If you would like further information on standard detail, notation, and other A/E management checklists and software, contact:

GUIDELINES
Box 456
Orinda, CA 94563

(415) 254-0639

1.0

GENERAL INFORMATION--WORKING DRAWING SHEET FORMAT AND CONTENT

Standard architectural sheet sizes: 18" x 24", 24" x 36", 30" x 42".

Standard engineering sheet sizes: A = 8-1/2" x 11", B = 11" x 17", C = 17" x 22", D = 22" x 34", E = 34" x 44".

Standard margins: 1-1/2" left-hand binder margin, 1/2" at top, bottom, and right-hand side.

1/2" or more trim space around outer border of sheets. (This is a way to eliminate edge damage prior to final printing.)

Drawing sheets created at double size for later photo reduction and 50% size printing usually start at 30" x 42" or 34" x 44"; they reduce to final sizes of 15" x 21" and 17" x 22" (or less if sheets are trimmed).

Recommended maximum drawing size: To meet limits of microfilm blowback system at bidding pools, maximum size may be 30" x 42".

IN   OK

____ ____   TITLE BLOCKS AT LOWER RIGHT OR DOWN RIGHT-HAND SIDE OF DRAWING

____ ____   GENERAL NOTES AND/OR KEYNOTE STRIP 3" TO 4" WIDE ON RIGHT-HAND SIDE (Size varies depending on overall drawing module you use.)

____ ____   DETAIL MODULE RECOMMENDED: 5-3/4" HIGH x 6" LONG CAN BE AD-JUSTED TO FIT MOST STANDARD DRAWING SHEET SIZES WHEN USED IN COMBINATION WITH VARIABLE SIZE RIGHT-HAND TITLE BLOCKS AND/OR KEYNOTE STRIPS

____ ____   SCHEDULE ON LEFT-HAND TRIM MARGIN TO RECORD DATES AND TIMES OF WORK PERIODS ON SHEET BY INDIVIDUAL STAFF MEMBERS (This may be recorded separately on drawing schedule sheets such as those included with this manual.)

____ ____   TICK MARKS PRINTED AT BORDER EDGES TO GUIDE FOLDING OF DRAWINGS INTO APPROXIMATE 8-1/2" X 11" PACKETS FOR MAILING OR STORAGE

____ ____   TICK MARKS AT CENTERS OF ALL BORDER LINES TO GUIDE PHOTOGRAPHY

____ ____   GRAPHIC SCALE (Some drawings are noted at original scale with an added note that some final print sets may be at a reduced size. When all final prints are at reduced size, it's common to note only the final scale on the "double size" original sheet instead of making any reference to reduced sizes.)

GENERAL INFORMATION--TITLE BLOCK CONTENT Continued

IN   OK

___ ___   PRIME DESIGN FIRM'S NAME, ADDRESS AND PHONE

___ ___   ASSOCIATED OR JOINT VENTURE FIRM NAMES, ADDRESSES, PHONE
          NUMBERS

___ ___   REGISTRATION NUMBERS OR OFFICIAL STAMPS OF PRIME AND ASSOCIATED
          FIRMS

___ ___   PROJECT NAME AND ADDRESS

___ ___   OWNER'S NAME AND ADDRESS

___ ___   CONSULTANTS' REGISTRATION NUMBERS, NAMES, ADDRESSES AND PHONE
          NUMBERS (Include on title block if list is small. Other-
          wise list all data on the General Information sheet.)

___ ___   DRAWING TITLE AND SCALE

___ ___   MINI KEY PLAN OF BUILDING

___ ___   CONTACT PEOPLE IN THE PRIMARY DESIGN FIRM (These data may be
          on the General Information sheet instead of the title block.)
          ___ principal in charge
          ___ chief or project architect
          ___ job or team captain
          ___ office phone number and extension, plus alternate or after
              hours phone number of primary contact for client, bidders
              and contractor

___ ___   DESIGNERS AND DRAFTERS (A growing preference is to provide full
          names of job participants on the General Information sheet as
          well as the usual specific staff initials on individual sheets.)

___ ___   INITIALS OR NAME OF DRAWING CHECKER

___ ___   SPACE FOR REVISION DATES AND REVISION REFERENCE SYMBOLS

___ ___   PROJECT NUMBER

___ ___   FILE NUMBER

___ ___   SPACE FOR GENERAL NOTES (General notes are usually placed in
          a separate note or keynote strip on the right-hand side.)

___ ___   COPYRIGHT NOTICE OR NOTE ON RIGHTS AND RESTRICTIONS OF
          OWNERSHIP AND USE OF DRAWINGS

GENERAL INFORMATION--TITLE BLOCK CONTENT Continued

IN   OK

___ ___ BUILDING AND PLANNING PERMIT AUTHORITIES, ADDRESSES AND PHONE
        NUMBERS

___ ___ PERMIT NUMBERS

___ ___ SPACE FOR APPROVAL STAMPS OR INITIALS

___ ___ DATES OF APPROVAL

___ ___ PRIVATE BUILDING CODE CHECKING SERVICE

___ ___ CHECKING DATES

___ ___ JOB PHASE COMPLETION DATES

___ ___ CLIENT APPROVALS

___ ___ FINAL RELEASE DATE

___ ___ DRAWING SHEET NUMBER AND TOTAL NUMBER OF DRAWINGS

___ ___ SHEET NUMBER CODING FOR DRAWINGS OF DIFFERENT CONSULTANTS

___ ___ CODING FOR SEPARATE BUILDINGS OR PORTIONS OF PROJECT

COVER SHEETS/INDEX SHEETS

IN   OK

___ ___ PROJECT NAME

___ ___ OWNER'S NAME

___ ___ PRIME DESIGN FIRM

___ ___ ASSOCIATED OR JOINT VENTURE DESIGN FIRMS

___ ___ PERSPECTIVE RENDERING OR PHOTO OF MODEL (Some firms now use
        photos of people such as users of the building, clients,
        or the design team.)

GENERAL INFORMATION--COVER SHEETS/INDEX SHEETS Continued

IN   OK

____ ____ CONSULTANTS (Names, addresses and phone numbers. Include on
title block if list is small. Otherwise list all consultants
and related data on the General Information sheet.)

     ____ structural

     ____ hvac

     ____ plumbing

     ____ electrical

     ____ lighting design

     ____ soils

     ____ civil

     ____ landscaping

     ____ interiors

     ____ acoustical

     ____ auditorium

     ____ kitchen/food service

     ____ design management

     ____ construction management

     ____ energy

     ____ solar

     ____ fire safety

     ____ barrier-free handicap access

____ ____ INDEX OF ARCHITECTURAL AND CONSULTANTS' DRAWINGS

____ ____ GENERAL NOTES

____ ____ LEXICON OF ABBREVIATIONS AND NOMENCLATURE

GENERAL INFORMATION--COVER SHEETS/INDEX SHEETS   Continued

IN   OK

____ ____   LEGEND OF CONSTRUCTION MATERIALS INDICATIONS AND DRAWING
            CONVENTIONS

____ ____   LEGEND OF SITEWORK, STRUCTURAL, ELECTRICAL, PLUMBING, AND HVAC
            SYMBOLS AND CONVENTIONS   (If not shown on other drawings.)

____ ____   LEGEND OF SYMBOLS:

            ____ elevation point

            ____ level line

            ____ revisions

            ____ column or module grid key

            ____ building cross section or partial section key

            ____ wall section key

            ____ detail key

            ____ window number key to window schedule

            ____ door symbol key to schedule

            ____ room or area number key to finish schedule

            ____ stair key

            ____ equipment key

            ____ existing work, work to be removed, new work

____ ____   EXPLANATION OF SYSTEMS DRAFTING COMPONENTS

            ____ keynote system

            ____ fixture heights schedules instead of interior elevations

            ____ simplified door, window, finish schedule, and detail keys

            ____ wall construction schedule key symbol if wall materials
                 indications aren't shown

            ____ explanation of screened shadow print background printing

CHAPTER TWO--SITE PLANS   2.0 - 2.30

SITE PLANS--INTRODUCTION

A typical site plan shows a building outline or "footprint" (or the
ground floor plan) in combination with paving, landscaping, site furniture, and auxiliary construction. Since grading, drainage, sewer-
age, paving, electrical, finish landscaping, and other work are often
let as separate subcontracts, a series of sitework drawings may be
necessary to sufficiently separate out the different types and layers
of work. The checklist that follows is divided accordingly.

ITEMS THAT SHOULD BE AVOIDED ON SITEWORK DRAWINGS

____ The site survey is often traced or redrawn from scratch. This is
done either to change its scale from an engineering scale to the
architectural site plan scale, or to enhance an otherwise badly
drawn survey, or because all that's available is an old nonrepro-
ducible print. None of these reasons are justified for this very
time-consuming operation. See the Systems Drafting section on
page 2.2 for alternatives.

____ Foliage and ground cover tend to be overdrawn. Simple outline indications are more readable, and they reduce the chances of obscur-
ing or crowding out other data.

COORDINATION

____ The first and most important coordination device is a double check
on the accuracy of the survey. Surveys are very often in error.
All major features should be checked and measured on the site before
starting any design or feasibility studies. For projects of significant scope, obtain aerial or satellite photos of the site. Have
them made to working drawing scale for overlay comparison with the
engineer's survey. Aerial photos are commonly available as photo
washoff or contact print reproducible translucencies to expedite
reproduction and overlay work. (Because of angular distortion common to most aerial photo views, the overlay match with a survey
plan will not be precisely accurate. But it will allow review of
major features in the photo that may or may not be shown accurately
on the survey.)

____ Instruct the client to have the survey drawn and printed at an architectural scale so that it will be directly reusable by the design firm. Have it printed on a reproducible medium such as photo-
washoff or sepia diazo polyester film.

SITE PLANS--INTRODUCTION Continued

COORDINATION Continued

____ Use overlay comparisons of all sitework plans to correlate trenching for foundations, utility lines, grading and landscaping work.

____ Compare the site plan with the (usually larger scale) roof plan
to coordinate site drainage and building drainage.

ITEMS SUITED TO SYSTEMS DRAFTING, PASTE-UP, AND OVERLAY

____ As cited above, have the original survey provided at a usable
scale and as a reproducible print on polyester film. After making
appropriate revisions, make a screened shadow print of the survey
as a contour map background sheet or base sheet for further work.

____ If only a print of the survey is available--possibly damaged, or
at the wrong scale--it can be turned into a clean and/or resized
reproducible through photo-washoff reproduction. If the scale is
all right, you can possibly get a usable reproducible from a paper
print on diazo sepia line polyester through extended exposure on
a vacuum frame. Another alternative is to use a large format reduction copier such as Xerox 2080 to clean, alter scale, and
create a reproducible from an opaque print.

____ Make a floor plan outline or "footprint" of the building and apply
a copy as a paste-up on an overlay atop the survey contour map base
sheet. Or you can have the ground floor plan photoreduced to site
plan scale and use it as the paste-up. This latter alternative is
often helpful for accurately routing utilities, drains and sewers
to their best hookup points at the building.

____ Paving, parking patterns, and ground textures can be added as
stickyback appliques or clear film paste-ups. Use graphic pattern
tapes for boundary lines, fencing, cut lines, etc.

____ Make new reproducible prints showing the survey as a screened shadow print and the building and related construction in solid line.
Distribute them to consultants as base sheets.

____ In final printing, consider showing each sitework contract as a
solid line image combined with a multi-layer screened shadow print
of all other contracts. That is, trenching for the water lines is
printed as solid on one sheet while all other work is screened.
Drainage and storm sewers are solid on another sheet with all other
contracts shown in screened image, and so on. This shows all sub-
contractors how their work may be coordinated with others and where
potential points of overlap and conflict may exist. That helps a-
void delays from duplicate excavations and/or trenching into previously installed underground utilities.

SITE PLANS--INTRODUCTION   Continued

ITEMS SUITED TO SYSTEMS DRAFTING, PASTE-UP, AND OVERLAY   Continued

____ All sitework drawings--Landscaping, Grading, Site Improvements, etc.--are well suited to keynoting. Use keynote strip legends at the right side of the drawings, and bubble-reference all notes to the legend. Site construction detail references can also be linked to the keynote legend as a further coordination device. If landscape drawings include large numbers of repetitive and lengthy Latin botanical terms, they should certainly be keynoted.

____ In lieu of keynoting, you can type or computer print one or more strips of notes and copy them as stickybacks or translucent paste-up elements.

____ Photograph any special site features such as rock outcrops, trees requiring special protection, existing work to be removed, etc. Include the photos adjacent to site plans with added linework and notation. Use graphic tape leader lines or number keys to link the photo subjects to their actual positions on the site.

____ Sitework, drainage, paving, and landscaping details are very standard. Most such detailing on most projects could be provided from an office's standard or reference detail library.

____ Foliage designs and patterns are widely available as applique dry transfer rub-ons and stickybacks. You can also make your own library of patterns and foliage designs and copy them in multiple onto clear films for paste-up.

____ Symbol legends, general notes, north arrows, drawing titles, and all other such repeat elements can be standardized and printed on clear films to use for paste-ups.

____ Engineering symbols and the large variety of symbolic linework used in site drawings are especially suited to small unit rub-on or pre-cut stickyback appliques and drafting with graphic tape.

SITE PLANS--CHECKLIST OF SITE PLAN DRAWINGS

Site plans may incorporate individual or combined sheets, including the following:

IN   OK

___ ___   SURVEY

___ ___   STAKING PLAN

___ ___   TEST PIT AND BORING PLAN

___ ___   GRADING PLAN

___ ___   DEMOLITION PLAN

___ ___   EXCAVATION PLAN

___ ___   CONSTRUCTION WORK AND TEMPORARY FACILITIES

___ ___   ARCHITECTURAL SITE PLAN
             ___ general construction
             ___ paving, walkways and parking
             ___ site furniture and appurtenances

___ ___   DRAINAGE PLAN

___ ___   LANDSCAPING PLAN

___ ___   ELECTRICAL
             ___ supply
             ___ outdoor lighting

___ ___   HVAC

___ ___   PLUMBING
             ___ supply
             ___ irrigation
             ___ sprinkler

SITE PLANS--GENERAL REFERENCE INFORMATION

IN   OK

____ ____ DRAWING TITLE AND SCALE
____ ____ ARROWS SHOWING COMPASS NORTH AND REFERENCE NORTH
____ ____ SMALL-SCALE LOCATION OR VICINITY MAP SHOWING NEIGHBORING
           STREETS AND NEAREST MAJOR HIGHWAY ACCESS   (Can be applique or
           paste-up copy of a portion of the local road map.)
____ ____ NOTE REQUIRING BIDDERS TO VISIT SITE AND VERIFY CONDITIONS
           BEFORE SUBMITTING BIDS
____ ____ WORK NOT IN CONTRACT
____ ____ PROPERTY SIZE IN SQUARE FEET OR ACRES
____ ____ CONTRACT LIMIT LINES
____ ____ LOCATION AND SIZE DIMENSIONS OF CONSTRUCTED COMPONENTS
____ ____ DETAIL KEYS
____ ____ DRAWING CROSS REFERENCES
____ ____ SPECIFICATION REFERENCES
____ ____ LEGAL SETBACK LINES
____ ____ EASEMENTS
____ ____ SITE PHOTOS   (Usually printed adjacent to the site plan draw-
           ing with connecting arrow lead lines to show the exact areas
           of site represented by photos.)
____ ____ LEGENDS OF SITE PLAN SYMBOLS AND MATERIAL INDICATIONS
____ ____ LANDSCAPE CONSULTANT
              ____ address and phone number

____ ____ SURVEYOR
              ____ address and phone number
              ____ registration number

____ ____ CIVIL ENGINEER
              ____ address and phone number
              ____ registration number

____ ____ SOILS ENGINEER
              ____ address and phone number
              ____ registration number

____ ____ SOIL TEST LAB
              ____ address and phone number
              ____ registration number

____ ____ TEST BORING CONTRACTOR
              ____ address and phone number

____ ____ DESCRIPTION OF SOIL TYPE AND BEARING
____ ____ PERCOLATION TEST PLAN
____ ____ SOILS TESTING BORING SCHEDULE AND PROFILE
____ ____ TEST BORING LOCATIONS
____ ____ BORING TEST PROFILE FROM SOILS ENGINEER
           (May be separate drawing.)

SITE PLANS--CONSTRUCTION WORK AND TEMPORARY FACILITIES

Most or all of these items will be designed and located by the contractor as part of the construction contract.

IN   OK

___ ___   TEMPORARY EROSION CONTROL 01560 (01568/02270)
           ___ materials ___ dimensions ___ detail keys ___ notes/refs
           coord check: ___ civil/soil

___ ___   TEMPORARY RETAINING WALLS 01560 (01569/02151)
           ___ materials ___ dimensions ___ detail keys ___ notes/refs
           coord check: ___ civil/soil ___ struct

___ ___   SHORING 02150 (02151)
           ___ materials ___ dimensions ___ detail keys ___ notes/refs
           coord check: ___ civil/soil ___ struct

___ ___   TEMPORARY DRAINAGE 01560 (01563)
           ___ materials ___ dimensions ___ detail keys ___ notes/refs
           coord check: ___ civil/soil

___ ___   TEMPORARY FENCE/BARRICADE 01530 (01531)
           ___ materials ___ dimensions ___ detail keys ___ notes/refs
           coord check: ___ code

___ ___   FENCE/BARRICADE GATES 01530 (01531)
           ___ materials ___ dimensions ___ detail keys ___ notes/refs

___ ___   PROJECT SIGN 01580 (01580)
           ___ materials ___ dimensions ___ detail keys ___ notes/refs

___ ___   FIELD OFFICE 01590 (01590)
           ___ materials ___ dimensions ___ detail keys ___ notes/refs

___ ___   WATCHMAN'S STATION 01540 (01545/01590)
           ___ materials ___ dimensions ___ detail keys ___ notes/refs

___ ___   MAIN SECURITY GUARD STATION 01540 (01545)
           ___ materials ___ dimensions ___ detail keys ___ notes/refs

___ ___   SECURITY TIME CLOCK PUNCH STATION 01540 (01545)
           ___ locations ___ notes/refs

___ ___   FIRST AID STATIONS 01510 (01517)
           ___ locations ___ notes/refs
           coord check: ___ code

___ ___   TOILETS AND SANITATION 01510 (01516)
           ___ locations ___ notes/refs

SITE PLANS--CONSTRUCTION WORK AND TEMPORARY FACILITIES Continued

IN   OK

___ ___   BARRICADES 01530 (01533)
            ___ materials ___ dimensions ___ detail keys ___ notes/refs
            coord check: ___ code

___ ___   TEMPORARY BARRIERS OR PARTITIONS BETWEEN CONSTRUCTION AREAS
            AND OCCUPIED AREAS 01530 (01533)
            ___ materials ___ dimensions ___ detail keys ___ notes/refs

___ ___   TESTING AREA 01400 (01400)
            ___ dimensions ___ notes/refs

___ ___   SAMPLES STORAGE SHELTER 01600 (01620)
            ___ materials ___ dimensions ___ detail keys ___ notes/refs

___ ___   MATERIAL AND EQUIPMENT STORAGE AREAS 01600 (01620)
            ___ dimensions ___ notes/refs

___ ___   PLATFORMS 01500 (01519)
            ___ materials ___ dimensions ___ detail keys ___ notes/refs

___ ___   BRIDGES FOR PROTECTION OF PAVING, WALKS, CURBS FROM CONSTRUC-
            TION EQUIPMENT AND TRUCKS 01500 (01519)
            ___ materials ___ dimensions ___ detail keys ___ notes/refs
            coord check: ___ paving ___ util

___ ___   CONSTRUCTION CRANES
            ___ location ___ notes/refs
            coord check: ___ util

___ ___   TEMPORARY ROADS 01550 (01551)
            ___ materials ___ dimensions ___ notes/refs
            coord check: ___ civil/soils ___ site drain ___ util

___ ___   TEMPORARY PARKING 01550 (01552)
            ___ dimensions ___ notes/refs
            coord check: ___ civil/soils ___ site drain

___ ___   TEMPORARY WALKWAYS 01500 (01519)
            ___ materials ___ dimensions ___ notes/refs

___ ___   EXCAVATION SOIL STORAGE AREAS AND SPOIL AREAS 02200 (02200)
            ___ dimensions ___ notes/refs
            coord check: ___ civil/soils ___ landscape

___ ___   TOPSOIL STOCKPILE AREA 02480 (02484)
            ___ dimensions ___ notes/refs
            coord check: ___ civil/soils ___ landscape

SITE PLANS--CONSTRUCTION WORK AND TEMPORARY FACILITIES   Continued

IN   OK

_____ _____   PLANT STORAGE YARD   02480   (02482)
                 ____ dimensions ____ notes/refs
                 coord check: ____ landscape

_____ _____   PLANT STORAGE GREENHOUSE   02480   (02482)
                 ____ materials ____ dimensions ____ detail keys ____ notes/refs
                 coord check: ____ landscape

_____ _____   TREE AND PLANT PROTECTION   01500   (01532)
                 ____ locations ____ notes/refs
                 coord check: ____ landscape

_____ _____   CONSTRUCTION POWER POLE AND METER   01510   (01511)
                 ____ location ____ notes/refs
                 coord check: ____ elec

_____ _____   CONSTRUCTION TELEPHONE LINE AND POLES   01510   (01514)
                 ____ locations ____ notes/refs
                 coord check: ____ elec

_____ _____   SITE ILLUMINATION   01510   (01512)
                 ____ locations ____ notes/refs
                 coord check: ____ elec

_____ _____   CONSTRUCTION WATER SUPPLY HYDRANTS   01510   (01515)
                 ____ locations ____ notes/refs
                 coord check: ____ plumb

_____ _____   TEMPORARY HOSE BIBBS   01510   (01515)
                 ____ locations ____ notes/refs
                 coord check: ____ plumb

_____ _____   FIRE HOSE RACKS   01510/15500   (01518)
                 ____ locations ____ notes/refs
                 coord check: ____ code

_____ _____   WASTE CHUTE   01560   (01566)
                 ____ locations ____ notes/refs

_____ _____   TRASH AND DEBRIS STORAGE   01560   (01566)
                 ____ locations ____ notes/refs

_____ _____   SOIL TEST BORINGS   02010   (02011)
                 ____ locations ____ notes/refs
                 coord check: ____ civil/soils

_____ _____   SOIL TEST PITS   02010   (02011)
                 ____ locations ____ notes/refs
                 coord check: ____ civil/soils

SITE PLANS--DEMOLITION AND REPAIR

IN   OK

___ ___   EXISTING FENCES AND WALLS 02050 (02070)
          ___ to remain ___ to be repaired ___ to be removed

___ ___   EXISTING STRUCTURES 02050 (02060)
          ___ materials ___ dimensions ___ notes/refs
          ___ to remain ___ to be repaired ___ to be removed

___ ___   STRUCTURE MOVING 02100 (02120)

___ ___   ACCESS TO ADJACENT STRUCTURES 01550 (01550)

___ ___   PROTECTION FOR ADJACENT STRUCTURES

___ ___   EXISTING PAVING, WALKS, STEPS, AND CURBS 02050 (02070)
          ___ to remain ___ to be repaired ___ to be removed
          coord check: ___ paving ___ landscape

___ ___   CONCRETE REMOVAL 02200 (02212)

___ ___   ASBESTOS REMOVAL 02050 (02080)

___ ___   EXISTING ON-SITE UTILITIES, SEWERS, AND DRAINS 02050 (02070)
          ___ to remain ___ to be repaired ___ to be removed
          coord check: ___ util ___ site drain

___ ___   EXISTING TREES, SHRUBS, AND UNDERGROWTH 02100 (02111)
          ___ to remain ___ to be removed ___ to be relocated
          coord check: ___ landscape ___ util

___ ___   AREAS FOR CLEARING AND GRUBBING 02100 (02110)
          coord check: ___ landscape

___ ___   EXISTING TRASH TO BE REMOVED 01560 (01566)

___ ___   STUMPS TO BE REMOVED 02100 (02111)
          coord check: ___ landscape

___ ___   ROCK OUTCROPS TO REMAIN 02200 (02211)
          coord check: ___ util ___ landscape

___ ___   ROCK TO BE REMOVED 02200 (02211)
          coord check: ___ landscape

SITE PLANS--GRADING

IN   OK

___ ___   EXISTING AND NEW SITE CONTOURS 02200 (02260)
          coord check: ___ paving ___ landscape ___ site drain

___ ___   EXISTING AND NEW FINISH GRADES 02200 (02260)
          coord check: ___ paving ___ landscape ___ site drain

___ ___   ELEVATION POINTS 02200 (02260)
          coord check: ___ paving ___ landscape ___ site drain

___ ___   NEW BENCH MARK AND/OR BOUNDARY MARKERS

___ ___   EXISTING HOLES AND TRENCHES 02200 (02220/02221)
          ___ to remain ___ to be filled in
          coord check: ___ landscape ___ site drain ___ util

___ ___   NEW FILL 02200 (02210)
          coord check: ___ paving ___ landscape

___ ___   NOTE ON SOIL COMPACTION 02200 (02250)

___ ___   CUT AND FILL PROFILE 02200 (02210)
          (May be a separate drawing sheet.)

SITE PLANS--SITE DRAINAGE

IN   OK

___ ___   FRENCH DRAIN 02400 (02401)
            ___ materials ___ dimensions ___ detail keys ___ notes/refs
            ___ slopes ___ depths
           coord check: ___ civil/soil ___ util ___ paving ___ landsc

___ ___   PAVEMENT UNDERDRAIN 02400 (02410)
            ___ materials ___ dimensions ___ detail keys ___ notes/refs
            ___ slopes ___ depths
           coord check: ___ civil/soil ___ util ___ paving ___ landsc

___ ___   TRENCH DRAIN 02400 (02410)
            ___ materials ___ dimensions ___ detail keys ___ notes/refs
            ___ slopes ___ depths
           coord check: ___ civil/soil ___ util ___ paving ___ landsc

___ ___   SUBDRAINS 02400 (02410)
            ___ materials ___ dimensions ___ detail keys ___ notes/refs
            ___ slopes ___ depths
           coord check: ___ civil/soil ___ util ___ paving ___ landsc

___ ___   STORM DRAINS 02400 (02420)
            ___ materials ___ dimensions ___ detail keys ___ notes/refs
            ___ slopes ___ depths
           coord check: ___ civil/soil ___ util ___ paving ___ landsc

___ ___   AREA DRAINS 02400 (02420)
            ___ materials ___ dimensions ___ detail keys ___ notes/refs
            ___ slopes ___ depths
           coord check: ___ civil/soil ___ util ___ paving ___ landsc

___ ___   DRAINAGE FLUME/SPILLWAY 02400 (02420)
            ___ materials ___ dimensions ___ detail keys ___ notes/refs
            ___ slopes ___ depths
           coord check: ___ civil/soil ___ util ___ paving ___ landsc

___ ___   SLOTTED DRAINPIPE AND SLOT 02400 (02420)
            ___ materials ___ dimensions ___ detail keys ___ notes/refs
            ___ slopes ___ depths
           coord check: ___ civil/soil ___ util ___ paving ___ landsc

___ ___   DRAIN AT PAVING EDGE 02400 (02420)
            ___ materials ___ dimensions ___ detail keys ___ notes/refs
            ___ slopes ___ depths
           coord check: ___ paving

___ ___   CATCH BASINS 02400 (02431)
            ___ materials ___ dimensions ___ detail keys ___ notes/refs
            ___ slopes ___ depths
           coord check: ___ civil/soil ___ util ___ paving ___ landsc

SITE PLANS--SITE DRAINAGE Continued

IN   OK

___ ___   CURB INLETS 02400 (02432)
          ___ materials ___ dimensions ___ detail keys ___ notes/refs
          ___ slopes ___ depths
          coord check: ___ paving

___ ___   CULVERTS 02400 (02434)
          ___ materials ___ dimensions ___ detail keys ___ notes/refs
          ___ slopes ___ depths
          coord check: ___ civil/soil ___ util ___ paving ___ landsc

___ ___   EROSION CONTROL 02200 (02270)
          ___ materials ___ dimensions ___ detail keys ___ notes/refs
          coord check: ___ civil/soil ___ paving ___ landscape

___ ___   RIP RAP 02200 (02271)
          ___ materials ___ dimensions ___ detail keys ___ notes/refs
          ___ slopes ___ depths
          coord check: ___ civil/soil ___ paving ___ landscape

___ ___   HEAD WALLS 02400 (02420)
          ___ materials ___ dimensions ___ detail keys ___ notes/refs
          coord check: ___ civil/soil ___ util ___ paving ___ landsc

___ ___   DRY WELLS 02400 (02420)
          ___ materials ___ dimensions ___ detail keys ___ notes/refs
          coord check: ___ civil/soil ___ util ___ paving ___ lands

___ ___   BUILDING PERIMETER FOUNDATION DRAINAGE 02400 (02411)
          ___ slope
          ___ depths
          ___ direction of drain to dry well or storm sewer
          ___ materials ___ dimensions ___ detail keys ___ notes/refs
          coord check: ___ civil/soil ___ util

___ ___   BUILDING RAIN LEADER DRAINAGE 02400 (02430/15406)
          coord check: ___ roof drain ___ ext elev

___ ___   SURFACE OR DRIP DRAINAGE BELOW ROOF EDGES 02400 (02436)
          coord check: ___ roof drain ___ ext elev

___ ___   SPLASH BLOCKS 02400 (02435)
          ___ materials ___ dimensions ___ detail keys ___ notes/refs
          coord check: ___ roof drains ___ landscape ___ ext elev

SITE PLANS--SITEWORK CONSTRUCTION

IN   OK

___ ___   PORTIONS OF EXISTING STRUCTURES TO BE REMOVED 02050 (02070)
         ___ materials ___ dimensions ___ detail keys ___ notes/refs

___ ___   NEW BUILDING AND RELATED STRUCTURES
         ___ overall exterior wall dimensions
         ___ dimensions to property lines
         ___ outline of future building additions
         ___ building layout line
         ___ building finish floor elevation at ground floor or basement
         ___ materials ___ dimensions ___ detail keys ___ notes/refs
         coord check: ___ zoning ___ util ___ struct ___ civil/soils
              ___ site drain

___ ___   NEW FINISH GRADE ELEVATIONS AT BUILDING CORNERS 02200 (02260)
         coord check: ___ survey ___ civil ___ site drain

___ ___   GRADE SLOPE AT BUILDING LINE 02200 (02260)
         (Slope grade away from building on all sides.)
         coord check: ___ survey ___ civil ___ site drain

___ ___   FOUNDATION OR BASEMENT EXCAVATION LIMIT LINES 02200 (02220)
         coord check: ___ civil ___ struct

___ ___   RETAINING WALLS OR WELLS FOR EXISTING TREES AFFECTED BY
         CHANGES IN FINISH GRADE 02480 (02491)
         ___ materials ___ dimensions ___ detail keys ___ notes/refs
         ___ elevation points
         coord check: ___ landscape ___ civil/soil ___ struct

___ ___   FENCES AND GATES 02440
         ___ CHAIN LINK 02440 (02444)
         ___ WIRE 02440 (02445)
         ___ WOOD 02440 (02446)
         ___ METAL 02440 (02447)
         ___ heights or elevation points
         ___ gate swings
         ___ powered gates
         ___ fence and gate lights
         ___ alarms
         materials ___ dimensions ___ detail keys ___ notes/refs
         coord check: ___ ext elev ___ landscape ___ elec

SITE PLANS--SITEWORK CONSTRUCTION Continued

IN   OK

___ ___ YARD WALLS
         ___ CONCRETE 03300 (03300)
         ___ BRICK 04200 (04210)
         ___ CONCRETE BLOCK 04200 (04220)
         ___ STONE 04400 (04400)
         ___ heights or elevation points
         ___ wall lights
         ___ alarms
         ___ materials ___ dimensions ___ detail keys ___ notes/refs
         coord check: ___ ext elev ___ landscape ___ elec

___ ___ RETAINING WALLS
         ___ WOOD 02440 (02449)
         ___ CONCRETE 03300 (03302)
         ___ BRICK 04200 (04210)
         ___ CONCRETE BLOCK 04200 (04228)
         ___ STONE 04400 (04400)
         ___ materials ___ dimensions ___ detail keys ___ notes/refs
         ___ heights or elevation points
         coord check: ___ landscape ___ civil/soil ___ struct
              ___ site drain

___ ___ RETAINING WALL CONCRETE FOOTINGS 03300 (03305)
         ___ dimensions ___ detail keys ___ notes/refs
         ___ heights or elevation points
         coord check: ___ civil/soil ___ struct ___ site drain

___ ___ RETAINING WALL FOOTING DRAINAGE 02400 (02411)
         ___ materials ___ dimensions ___ detail keys ___ notes/refs
         ___ sizes ___ slopes ___ depths
         coord check: ___ civil/soil ___ struct ___ site drain

___ ___ RETAINING WALL RELIEF DRAINS OR WEEP HOLES 02400 (02415)
         ___ materials ___ dimensions ___ detail keys ___ notes/refs
         coord check: ___ site drain

SITE PLANS--APPURTENANCES AND SITE FURNITURE

Site furniture data is often included on the Landscaping Plan. Most
items can be assumed to require coordination checking with any separate landscaping drawings. See Landscaping, page 2.29.

The "paving" reference on the coordination checklists may refer both
to the location of paving relevant to the item of construction and to
necessary correlated anchors, curbs, pedestals, footings, etc.

IN   OK

___ ___   PONDS   02590   (02590)
          ___ materials ___ dimensions ___ detail keys ___ notes/refs
          coord check: ___ civil/soil ___ plumb ___ drain ___ paving

___ ___   SWIMMING/WADING POOLS   13150   (13151)
          (Nonslip paving.)
          ___ equipment
          ___ equipment enclosure
          ___ materials ___ dimensions ___ detail keys ___ notes/refs
          coord check: ___ civil/soil ___ plumb ___ drain ___ paving
          ___ elec

___ ___   FOUNTAINS   02440   (02443)
          (Fountains located away from wind channels.)
          ___ materials ___ dimensions ___ detail keys ___ notes/refs
          coord check: ___ civil/soil ___ plumb ___ drain ___ paving
          ___ elec

___ ___   PLANTERS
          ___ WOOD   02440   (02449)
          ___ CONCRETE   03300   (03303)
          ___ BRICK   04200   (04203)
          ___ CONCRETE BLOCK   04200   (04228)
          ___ STONE   04400   (04400)
          ___ materials ___ dimensions ___ detail keys ___ notes/refs
          coord check: ___ plumb ___ drain ___ paving

___ ___   PLANT TUBS   02440   (02474)
          ___ materials ___ dimensions ___ detail keys ___ notes/refs
          coord check: ___ plumb ___ drain

___ ___   PLANTER DRAINAGE   02400   (02415)
          ___ dimensions ___ detail keys ___ notes/refs
          coord check: ___ plumb ___ drain

___ ___   PEDESTALS, CURBS, OR SUPPORT SLABS   03300   (03337)
          ___ materials ___ dimensions ___ detail keys ___ notes/refs
          coord check: ___ struct/slab ___ paving

SITE PLANS--APPURTENANCES AND SITE FURNITURE Continued

IN   OK

___ ___   FREESTANDING DIRECTION SIGNS 02440/10400 (02452/10440)
            ___ location/size ___ detail keys ___ notes/refs
            coord check: ___ paving ___ elec

___ ___   FREESTANDING LOCATION-MAP STANDS 02440/10400 (02452/10412)
            ___ location/size ___ detail keys ___ notes/refs
            coord check: ___ paving ___ elec

___ ___   FREESTANDING DIRECTORIES 02440/10400 (02452/10411)
            ___ location/size ___ detail keys ___ notes/refs
            coord check: ___ paving ___ elec

___ ___   FREESTANDING BULLETIN BOARDS 02440/10400 (02452/10415)
            ___ location/size ___ detail keys ___ notes/refs
            coord check: ___ paving ___ elec

___ ___   KIOSKS 02440/10400 (02452/10416)
            ___ location/size ___ detail keys ___ notes/refs
            coord check: ___ ext elev ___ paving ___ elec

___ ___   WALKWAY AND PARKING LIGHT STANDARDS AND PEDESTALS 02440/16500
            (02458/16530)
            ___ location/size ___ detail keys ___ notes/refs
            coord check: ___ paving ___ elec

___ ___   BENCHES 02440 (02471)
            (Usually set 2' back from walkways.)
            ___ materials ___ dimensions ___ detail keys ___ notes/refs
            coord check: ___ paving ___ elec

___ ___   TABLES 02440 (02472)
            ___ materials ___ dimensions ___ detail keys ___ notes/refs
            coord check: ___ paving ___ elec

___ ___   TRASH RECEPTACLES 02440 (02475)
            ___ location/size ___ detail keys ___ notes/refs
            coord check: ___ paving

___ ___   ASH RECEPTACLES 02440 (02476)
            ___ location/size ___ detail keys ___ notes/refs
            coord check: ___ paving

___ ___   PERGOLAS, LATTICES, ARBORS, AND TRELLISES
            ___ CONCRETE 03400 (03450)
            ___ METAL 05700 (05725)
            ___ WOOD 06400 (06450)
            ___ materials ___ dimensions ___ detail keys ___ notes/refs
            coord check: ___ fl plan ___ ext elev ___ roof ___ landscape
            ___ elec

SITE PLANS--APPURTENANCES AND SITE FURNITURE Continued

IN   OK

___ ___   COVERED WALKWAYS 10530 (10531)
            ___ materials ___ dimensions ___ detail keys ___ notes/refs
            coord check: ___ fl plan ___ ext elev ___ roof ___ landscape
            ___ elec

___ ___   DRINKING FOUNTAINS, AT EXTERIOR WALL 02440 (02479)
            ___ location/size ___ detail keys ___ notes/refs
            coord check: ___ fl plan ___ ext elev ___ paving ___ plumb
            ___ drain

___ ___   FREESTANDING DRINKING FOUNTAINS 02440 (02479)
            ___ location/size ___ detail keys ___ notes/refs
            coord check: ___ paving ___ plumb ___ drain

___ ___   HANDICAP DRINKING FOUNTAINS 02440 (02479)
            ___ location/size ___ detail keys ___ notes/refs
            coord check: ___ code ___ paving ___ plumb ___ drain

___ ___   CHILDREN'S LOW HEIGHT DRINKING FOUNTAINS 02440 (02479)
            ___ location/size ___ detail keys ___ notes/refs
            coord check: ___ paving ___ plumb ___ drain

___ ___   PET DRINKING FOUNTAINS 02440 (02479)
            ___ location/size ___ detail keys ___ notes/refs
            coord check: ___ paving ___ plumb ___ drain

___ ___   PAVEMENT DRAINS AT DRINKING FOUNTAINS 02400 (02420)
            ___ location/size ___ detail keys ___ notes/refs
            coord check: ___ paving ___ plumb ___ drain

___ ___   BICYCLE RACKS 02440 (02457)
            ___ location/size ___ detail keys ___ notes/refs
            coord check: ___ paving

___ ___   PRAM RACKS 02440 (02466)
            ___ location/size ___ detail keys ___ notes/refs
            coord check: ___ paving

___ ___   NEWSPAPER RACKS 02440 (02476)
            ___ location/size ___ notes/refs
            coord check: ___ paving

___ ___   TELEPHONE BOOTHS 02400/10750/16700 (02478/10751/16740)
            ___ location/size ___ detail keys ___ notes/refs
            coord check: ___ paving ___ elec

SITE PLANS--APPURTENANCES AND SITE FURNITURE Continued

IN   OK

___ ___   EMERGENCY PHONES 10750/16700 (10754/16740)
             ___ locations ___ detail keys ___ notes/refs
             coord check: ___ paving ___ elec

___ ___   LOW PHONES FOR HANDICAPPED OR CHILDREN 10750 (10755)
             ___ locations ___ detail keys ___ notes/refs
             coord check: ___ paving ___ elec

___ ___   FIRE ALARM BOXES 16700 (16721)
             ___ locations ___ notes/refs
             coord check: ___ code ___ paving ___ elec

___ ___   PUBLIC MAILBOXES 10550 (10552)
             ___ slot for handicapped
             ___ locations ___ detail keys ___ notes/refs
             coord check: ___ paving

___ ___   FLAGPOLES 10350 (10352)
             ___ location/size ___ detail keys ___ notes/refs
             coord check: ___ paving ___ elec

___ ___   BUS OR SHUTTLE STOP 02440 (02477)
             ___ benches
             ___ signs
             ___ shelter
             ___ waste receptacle
             ___ newspaper rack
             ___ materials ___ dimensions ___ detail keys ___ notes/refs
             coord check: ___ paving ___ ext elev ___ elec

___ ___   ROTARY GATES 10450 (10454)
             ___ location/size ___ detail keys ___ notes/refs
             coord check: ___ paving

___ ___   TURNSTILES 10450 (10456)
             ___ location/size ___ detail keys ___ notes/refs
             coord check: ___ paving

___ ___   DETECTION SPECIALTIES 10450 (10458)
             ___ location/size ___ detail keys ___ notes/refs
             coord check: ___ paving ___ elec

___ ___   INFORMATION OR GUARD BOOTH 02440 (02473/02478)
             ___ materials ___ dimensions ___ detail keys ___ notes/refs
             coord check: ___ paving ___ ext elev ___ elec

SITE PLANS--APPURTENANCES AND SITE FURNITURE   Continued

IN   OK

___ ___   PARKING EQUIPMENT   11150
            ___   PARKING GATE   11150   (11151)
            ___   TICKET DISPENSER   11150   (11152)
            ___   KEY AND CARD CONTROL UNIT   11150   (11153)
            ___   COIN MACHINE UNIT   11150   (11154)
            ___   TIRE SPIKE BARRIER   11150   (11159)
            ___ materials ___ dimensions ___ detail keys ___ notes/refs
            coord check: ___ paving

___ ___   PARKING ATTENDANT SHED   02440   (02473/02478)
            ___ materials ___ dimensions ___ detail keys ___ notes/refs
            coord check: ___ paving ___ ext elev ___ elec

___ ___   TRASH YARD AND ENCLOSURE   02440   (See Walls/Fences in "Sitework
            Construction.")
            ___ materials ___ dimensions ___ detail keys ___ notes/refs
            coord check: ___ paving ___ ext elev ___ plumb ___ drain
                  ___ elec

___ ___   MAINTENANCE YARD AND ENCLOSURE   02440   (See Walls/Fences in
            "Sitework Construction.")
            ___ storage racks
            ___ shelters or storage sheds
            ___ fuel storage tanks
            ___ fuel tank inlet, valve and pump
            ___ materials ___ dimensions ___ detail keys ___ notes/refs
            coord check: ___ paving ___ ext elev ___ plumb ___ drain
                  ___ elec

___ ___   PLAY FIELDS   02440   (02460)
            ___ materials ___ dimensions ___ detail keys ___ notes/refs
            coord check: ___ civil/soil ___ drain

___ ___   FENCED PLAY YARD   02440   (02460)
            ___ materials ___ dimensions ___ detail keys ___ notes/refs
            coord check: ___ paving ___ drain

___ ___   PLAYGROUND EQUIPMENT   02440   (02461)
            ___ location/size ___ detail keys ___ notes/refs
            coord check: ___ paving

___ ___   GAZEBO, GREENHOUSE, LATH HOUSE, STORAGE SHED   02440
            ___ materials ___ dimensions ___ detail keys ___ notes/refs
            coord check: ___ landscape ___ paving ___ plumb ___ elec

SITE PLANS--UTILITIES

IN   OK

___ ___   UTILITY CONNECT POINTS TO EXISTING MAINS 02700 (02710)
          ___ elevation points
          ___ locations ___ detail keys ___ notes/refs
          coord check: ___ survey

___ ___   MANHOLES AND CLEANOUTS 02600 (02601)
          ___ elevation points
          ___ materials ___ dimensions ___ detail keys ___ notes/refs
          coord check: ___ civil/soil ___ drain

___ ___   WATER SUPPLY MAIN 02700 (02713)
          ___ elevation points
          ___ location markers
          ___ materials ___ dimensions ___ detail keys ___ notes/refs
          coord check: ___ civil/soil ___ plumb ___ gas ___ steam
               ___ sewer ___ drain ___ elec

___ ___   WATER METERS 02700/15050 (02713/15181)
          ___ enclosure
          ___ location ___ notes/refs
          coord check: ___ plumb ___ paving

___ ___   WATER SHUTOFF BOX AND COVER 02700/15050 (02713/15181)
          ___ location ___ detail keys ___ notes/refs
          coord check: ___ plumb ___ paving

___ ___   FIRE HYDRANTS 02600/15500 (02644/15530)
          ___ locations ___ notes/refs
          coord check: ___ code ___ plumb ___ paving

___ ___   HOSE BIBBS 02600 (02640)
          ___ locations ___ notes/refs
          coord check: ___ plumb ___ landscape

___ ___   STANDPIPES 15500 (15530)
          ___ identifying markers for fire department
          ___ locations ___ detail keys ___ notes/refs
          coord check: ___ code ___ plumb ___ paving

___ ___   STEAM MAIN 15600 (15602)
          ___ materials ___ dimensions ___ detail keys ___ notes/refs
          coord check: ___ civil/soil ___ hvac ___ sewer ___ water
               ___ drain ___ elec ___ phone ___ tv

SITE PLANS--UTILITIES Continued

IN   OK

____ ____ GAS MAIN 02700 (02711)
           ____ elevation points
           ____ location markers
           ____ dimensions ____ detail keys ___ notes/refs
           coord check: ___ civil/soil ___ hvac ___ sewer ___ steam
                 ___ water ___ drain ___ elec

____ ____ GAS METERS 02700/15050 (02711/15182)
           ____ enclosure
           ____ location ___ detail keys ___ notes/refs
           coord check: ___ paving

____ ____ GAS SHUTOFF VALVE AT BUILDING 02600/02700 (02640/02711)
           ____ conspicuous location for shutoff, with identifying sign
           ____ lighting
           ____ location ___ notes/refs
           coord check: ___ paving ___ elec

____ ____ EXTERIOR ELECTRICAL OUTLETS 16050 (16134)
           ____ locations ___ notes/refs
           coord check: ___ paving

____ ____ EXTERIOR LIGHTS AT BUILDING AND AUXILIARY STRUCTURES
           16500 (16520)
           ____ locations ___ notes/refs
           coord check: ___ paving ___ ext elev ___ landscape

____ ____ OVERHEAD CABLES
           (Overhead cables to clear walks, driveways, trees, and
            structures.)
           ____ ELECTRICAL 02800 (02811)
           ____ COMMUNICATION 02800 (02820)
           ____ TELEPHONE 02800 (02821)
           ____ TV 02800 (02823)
           ____ locations ___ notes/refs
           coord check: ___ landscape ___ paving ___ ext elev

____ ____ BURIED CABLES
           ____ COMMUNICATION/FIBER OPTICS 02800 (02820)
           ____ ELECTRICAL 02800 (02812)
           ____ TELEPHONE 02800 (02821)
           ____ TV 02800 (02823)
           ____ elevation points
           ____ location markers
           ____ locations ___ detail keys ___ notes/refs
           coord check: ___ civil/soil ___ gas ___ water ___ steam
                 ___ drain ___ sewer

SITE PLANS--UTILITIES Continued

IN   OK

___ ___   SATELLITE DISH ANTENNA 11800/16700 (11800/16781)
            ___ antenna platform
            ___ enclosure
            ___ materials ___ dimensions ___ detail keys ___ notes/refs
            coord check: ___ paving ___ elec

___ ___   ELECTRICAL METERS 16400 (16430)
            ___ enclosure
            ___ location ___ detail keys ___ notes/refs
            coord check: ___ paving ___ elec

___ ___   TELEPHONE AND POWER POLES 02800 (02802)
            (Overhead cables to clear walks, driveways, trees, and
             structures.)
            ___ materials ___ locations ___ detail keys ___ notes/refs
            coord check: ___ paving ___ landscape ___ ext elev

___ ___   SERVICE ENTRANCES 16400 (16420)
            ___ locations ___ detail keys ___ notes/refs
            coord check: ___ fl plan ___ ext elev ___ roof

___ ___   TRANSFORMERS 16400 (16460)
            ___ vault
            ___ materials ___ locations ___ detail keys ___ notes/refs
            coord check: ___ paving ___ struct ___ drain

___ ___   UTILITY TRENCHES 02200 (02221)
            (Minimum and maximum depth limits.)
            ___ locations ___ notes/refs
            coord check: ___ civil/soil ___ landscape

___ ___   TRENCHING LOCATED TO AVOID DAMAGE TO TREE ROOTS AND NEIGHBORING
            STRUCTURES 02200 (02221)
            coord check: ___ civil/soil ___ landscape

___ ___   EXCAVATION WARNING SIGNS/MARKERS ALONG ROUTES OF BURIED UTILITY
            LINES 02440 (02452)
            ___ locations/sizes ___ detail keys ___ notes/refs
            coord check: ___ code ___ survey

___ ___   WATER WELL AND PUMP HOUSING 02700 (02730)
            ___ locations/sizes ___ detail keys ___ notes/refs
            coord check: ___ plumb ___ elec ___ sewer ___ drain

___ ___   CISTERNS 02700 (02720)
            ___ materials ___ dimensions ___ detail keys ___ notes/refs
            coord check: ___ civil/soil ___ plumb ___ sewer ___ drain

SITE PLANS--UTILITIES Continued

IN   OK

___ ___ FUEL OIL OR LIQUIFIED GAS STORAGE 13410 (13410)
          ___ storage tank
          ___ fuel line to building
          ___ vent
          ___ gauge box
          ___ fill box
          ___ manhole
          ___ materials ___ dimensions ___ detail keys ___ notes/refs
          coord check: ___ code ___ civil/soil ___ hvac

___ ___ SEWER MAIN 02700 (02722)
          ___ vent and cleanout
          ___ direction of slope
          ___ elevation points
          ___ location markers
          coord check: ___ civil/soil ___ gas ___ steam ___ water
               ___ drain ___ elec

___ ___ PACKAGE SEWAGE TREATMENT TANK AND HOUSING 02700 (02722)
          ___ materials ___ dimensions ___ detail keys ___ notes/refs
          coord check: ___ code ___ civil/soil ___ struct ___ plumb
               ___ elec ___ drain

___ ___ SEPTIC SYSTEM 02700 (02740)
          ___ septic tank
          ___ siphon tank
          ___ distribution boxes
          ___ seepage pit
          ___ leaching field
          ___ materials ___ dimensions ___ detail keys ___ notes/refs
          coord check: ___ code ___ civil/soil ___ landscape ___ plumb
               ___ drain

2.24

SITE PLANS--PAVING, WALKWAYS, AND PARKING

IN   OK

___ ___   EXTERIOR PARKING LOCATED MINIMUM 5' FROM WALLS AND OTHER
          STRUCTURES 02500

___ ___   PARKING SPACES LOCATED OUTSIDE TREE DRIP LINES 02500
          coord check: ___ landscape

___ ___   PARKING SPACES LOCATED OUTSIDE OF ICICLE OR ROOF SNOW DROP LINES

___ ___   WIDE SPACE PARKING FOR HANDICAPPED
          ___ HANDICAP PARKING PAVING SYMBOL 02500 (02577)
          ___ HANDICAP PARKING SIGN 02440 (02452)
          ___ HANDICAP RAMP 02440 (02458)
          coord check: ___ code

___ ___   TACTILE WARNING SURFACES FOR THE BLIND 02500 (02539)
          ___ materials ___ dimensions ___ detail keys ___ notes/refs

___ ___   NEW PUBLIC CURBS AT DRIVEWAY ENTRIES 02500
          ___ GRANITE 02500 (02525)
          ___ PRECAST 02500 CONCRETE (02526)
          ___ ASPHALT 02500 (02527)
          ___ CONCRETE 02500 (02528)
          ___ dimensions ___ detail keys ___ notes/refs
          ___ elevation points
          coord check: ___ civil/soil ___ site drain

___ ___   DRIVEWAYS 02500
          ___ CRUSHED STONE 02500 (02511)
          ___ ASPHALTIC CONCRETE 02500 (02513)
          ___ BRICK 02500 (02514)
          ___ CONCRETE 02500 (02515)
          ___ ASPHALT BLOCK 02500 (02516)
          ___ STONE 02500 (02517)
          ___ CONCRETE BLOCK 02500 (02518)
          ___ dimensions ___ detail keys ___ notes/refs
          ___ elevation points ___ slopes
          coord check: ___ civil/soil ___ site drain ___ landscape

___ ___   EXISTING AND NEW GRADE ELEVATIONS AT PAVING, NOTED AT CENTER
          LINES AND SIDES OF DRIVEWAYS 02500
          coord check: ___ civil/soil

___ ___   CROSS SECTION DIAGRAMS THROUGH ROADWAYS OR DRIVEWAYS 02500
          coord check: ___ civil/soil ___ site drain

___ ___   DRIVEWAY DRAINS 02400 (02420)
          ___ materials ___ dimensions ___ detail keys ___ notes/refs
          ___ elevation points ___ slopes
          coord check: ___ civil/soil ___ site drain

SITE PLANS--PAVING, WALKWAYS, AND PARKING Continued

IN   OK

___ ___   DRIVEWAY AND PARKING AREA GRADES 02500
          (Minimum 1/2%, maximum 5% at crowns)
          coord check: ___ civil/soil ___ site drain

___ ___   PAVEMENT AND WALKWAY ICE MELTING EQUIPMENT 15700/16850
          (15701/16858)
          ___ location/size ___ detail keys ___ notes/refs
          coord check: ___ elec

___ ___   ASPHALT PAVEMENT HUMPS 02500 (02516)
          ___ material ___ locations ___ detail keys ___ notes/refs

___ ___   WARNING SIGNS TO SLOW THROUGH TRAFFIC 02440 (02452)
          ___ locations ___ detail keys ___ notes/refs

___ ___   TRAFFIC CONTROL LIGHT STANDARDS 02440 (02453)
          ___ locations ___ detail keys ___ notes/refs
          coord check: ___ elec

___ ___   LOCKABLE POSTS OR CHAIN BARRIERS AT RESTRICTED ACCESS
          02440 (02450)
          ___ materials ___ dimensions ___ detail keys ___ notes/refs

___ ___   DRIVEWAY GATES 02440 (02444 to 02450)
          ___ materials ___ dimensions ___ detail keys ___ notes/refs

___ ___   DRIVEWAY FENCING 02440 (02444 to 02450)
          ___ materials ___ dimensions ___ detail keys ___ notes/refs

___ ___   PAVEMENT MARKING 02500 (02577)
          ___ parking spaces
          ___ handicapped parking
          ___ no parking areas
          ___ traffic control lines or markers
          ___ direction arrows
          ___ pedestrian crosswalks
          ___ pavement stop signs
          ___ slow or speed limit zones

___ ___   PARKING BUMPERS 02440 (02455/02456)
          ___ materials ___ dimensions ___ detail keys ___ notes/refs

___ ___   TRAFFIC CONTROL CURBS 02440 (02450)
          ___ materials ___ dimensions ___ detail keys ___ notes/refs

SITE PLANS--PAVING, WALKWAYS, AND PARKING   Continued

IN   OK

___ ___   PROTECTIVE VEHICULAR CURBS, BUMPERS, AND GUARD RAILINGS
           02440 (02450/02451 02455/02456)
           ___ garage entries
           ___ walls
           ___ ledges
           ___ walkways
           ___ steps
           ___ light standards
           ___ posts and columns
           ___ materials ___ dimensions ___ detail keys ___ notes/refs

___ ___   HANDICAP RAMP 02440 (02458)
           ___ materials ___ dimensions ___ detail keys ___ notes/refs
           coord check: ___ code

___ ___   CONSTRUCTION JOINTS IN CONCRETE PAVING 02500 (02515)
           (1/2" joints each 20' to 30' is typical, plus joints at connec-
           tions with other construction.)
           ___ materials ___ dimensions ___ detail keys ___ notes/refs
           coord check: ___ struct/slab

___ ___   RAMPS FROM PARKING AREA TO ADJACENT SIDEWALKS 02500
           ___ CRUSHED STONE 02500 (02511)
           ___ ASPHALTIC CONCRETE 02500 (02513)
           ___ BRICK 02500 (02514)
           ___ CONCRETE 02500 (02515)
           ___ ASPHALT BLOCK 02500 (02516)
           ___ STONE 02500 (02517)
           ___ CONCRETE BLOCK 02500 (02518)
           ___ dimensions ___ detail keys ___ notes/refs
           ___ elevation points ___ slopes
           coord check: ___ site drain ___ landscape

___ ___   WALKS 02500
           ___ WOOD PLANK 02500 (02506)
           ___ ASPHALTIC CONCRETE 02500 (02513)
           ___ BRICK 02500 (02514)
           ___ CONCRETE 02500 (02515)
           ___ ASPHALT 02500 (02516)
           ___ STONE 02500 (02517)
           ___ CONCRETE BLOCK/PAVERS 02500 (02518)
           ___ GRAVEL 02500 (02519)
           ___ dimensions ___ detail keys ___ notes/refs
           ___ elevation points ___ slopes
           coord check: ___ site drain ___ landscape

SITE PLANS--PAVING, WALKWAYS, AND PARKING Continued

IN   OK

____ ____   STEPS AT WALKS
            ____ BRICK 02500 (02514)
            ____ CONCRETE 02500 (02529)
            ____ STONE 02500 (02517)
            ____ CONCRETE BLOCK/PAVERS 02500 (02518)
            ____ WOOD 02500 (02523)
            ____ TILE FINISH 09300 (09300)
            ____ dimensions ___ detail keys ___ notes/refs
            ____ elevation points ___ slopes ___ riser number and heights
            coord check: ___ site drain

____ ____   BICYCLE AND PARAPLEGIC RAMPS ADJACENT TO WALKWAY STEPS
            AND AT CURBS 02440/02500 (02458/02510)
            ____ materials ___ dimensions ___ detail keys ___ notes/refs
            ____ elevation points ___ slopes
            coord check: ___ site drain

____ ____   HANDRAILS AT STEPS OVER 3 RISERS (05520/05521)
            ____ materials ___ dimensions ___ detail keys ___ notes/refs
            coord check: ___ code

____ ____   3 RISERS MINIMUM AT ANY POINT ALONG WALKS OR RAMPS 02500
            coord check: ___ code

____ ____   NONSKID SURFACES AT EXTERIOR WALKS, STEPS, AND LANDINGS 02500

____ ____   HANDRAILS AT SLOPING WALKS OR RAMPS 05500 (05520/05521)
            (Maximum slope for walkway without handrails is 1 in 8.)
            ____ materials ___ dimensions ___ detail keys ___ notes/refs
            coord check: ___ code

____ ____   PIPE SLEEVES IN PAVEMENT FOR FENCING OR RAILING POSTS
            02440 (02444 to 02446)
            ____ materials ___ dimensions ___ detail keys ___ notes/refs

____ ____   EXTERIOR STAIR, WALKWAY AND RAMP DRAINAGE 02400 (02420)
            ____ exterior stair identification numbers on plans
            ____ treads sloped to drain
            ____ side gutters at ramps, stairs, or steps
            ____ catch basins or drains at base of stairs or ramps
            ____ walkway low points sloped to drain
            ____ materials ___ dimensions ___ detail keys ___ notes/refs
            coord check: ___ civil/soil ___ site drain ___ landscape

____ ____   CONCRETE WALKWAY CONSTRUCTION JOINTS 02500 (02529)
            (1/2" joints each 30', tooled joints at 5'. Construction
            joints at connections with other construction.)
            ____ materials ___ dimensions ___ detail keys ___ notes/refs

SITE PLANS--PAVING, WALKWAYS, AND PARKING   Continued

IN   OK

___ ___   PAVED TERRACES AND PATIOS   02500
          (Open joint drainage or closed joint pavers. Solid paving
          sloped minimum 1" in 10' for drainage.)
              ___   BRICK   02500   (02514)
              ___   CONCRETE   02500   (02515)
              ___   STONE   02500   (02517)
              ___   CONCRETE BLOCK/PAVERS   02500   (02518)
              ___   TILE   09300   (09300)
              ___   WOOD DECKING   06100   (06125)
              ___   materials ___ dimensions ___ detail keys ___ notes/refs
              ___   elevation points ___ slopes
          coord check: ___ civil/soil ___ site drain ___ fl plan
                  ___ ext elev

___ ___   LAYOUT PATTERNS FOR PAVERS

___ ___   OPENINGS OR GRATINGS AT TREES IN PAVED AREAS FOR WATERING SPACE
          02480   (02491)
              ___ materials ___ dimensions ___ detail keys ___ notes/refs
          coord check: ___ landscape ___ site drain

___ ___   SYNTHETIC GRASS OR TURF   02500   (02541)
              ___ dimensions ___ notes/refs
          coord check: ___ site drain

___ ___   SIDEWALK GRATINGS   05500   (05530)
              ___ materials ___ dimensions ___ detail keys ___ notes/refs
          coord check: ___ util

___ ___   SIDEWALK ELECTRICAL VAULT   16300   (16301)
              ___ materials ___ dimensions ___ detail keys ___ notes/refs
          coord check: ___ elec ___ struct ___ util

___ ___   SIDEWALK PAVING GLASS IN PRECAST CONCRETE FOR UNDERGROUND ROOMS
          03400/04200   (03412/04270)
              ___ location/size ___ detail keys ___ notes/refs

___ ___   SIDEWALK ELEVATOR   14400   (14411)
              ___ location/size ___ detail keys ___ notes/refs
          coord check: ___ struct ___ elec

___ ___   ACCESS FOR FUEL DELIVERY   15600   (15605/15606)
              ___ location/size ___ detail keys ___ notes/refs
          coord check: ___ hvac

___ ___   SIDEWALK PLAQUES SPECIFYING PROPERTY OWNERSHIP AND LIMITS ON
          PUBLIC USE   10400   (10420)
              ___ materials ___ location/size ___ detail keys
              ___ notes/refs

SITE PLANS--LANDSCAPING

IN   OK

___ ___   EXISTING TREES, SHRUBS, AND UNDERGROWTH 01520/02100/02480
          (01532/02111/02481)
              ___ which to remain ___ which to remove
              ___ which to relocate and store for transplanting
              coord check: ___ demolition ___ const site

___ ___   TREES TO BE WRAPPED 01520/02480 (01532/02491)
          coord check: ___ const site

___ ___   TREE GUARDS FOR PROTECTION DURING CONSTRUCTION 01520 (01532)
              ___ materials ___ detail keys ___ notes/refs
              coord check: ___ const site

___ ___   NEW TOPSOIL STORAGE AREA 02480 (02483)
              ___ dimensions ___ notes/refs
              coord check: ___ const site

___ ___   EXCAVATION LOAM STORAGE AREA 02480 (02483)
              ___ dimensions ___ notes/refs
              coord check: ___ const site

___ ___   TEMPORARY EROSION CONTROL 01560/02200 (01568/02270)
              ___ materials ___ dimensions ___ detail keys ___ notes/refs
              coord check: ___ const site ___ site drain

___ ___   NEW LANDSCAPE DECORATIVE ROCK 02480 (02486)
              ___ location ___ notes/refs
              coord check: ___ civil/soil

___ ___   NEW LANDSCAPE AREA PLAN WITH LEGEND AND KEYS TO IDENTIFY TREES,
          PLANTS, AND GROUND COVER 02480 (02490)
              ___ all trees and shrubs shown at mature size
              ___ locations/sizes ___ notes/refs
              coord check: ___ civil/soil ___ util ___ plumb
              ___ site drain

___ ___   LAWN AND GRASS AREAS 02480 (02485)
              ___ dimensions ___ notes/refs
              coord check: ___ civil/soil ___ plumb ___ site drain

___ ___   SLOPES AND DRAINAGE FOR GROUND COVER AREAS 02400 (02420)
          coord check: ___ civil/soil ___ site drain

___ ___   ALL POCKETS AND STANDING WATER AREAS FILLED OR PROVIDED WITH
          DRAINAGE 02400 (02420)
              ___ materials ___ dimensions ___ detail keys ___ notes/refs
              coord check: ___ civil/soil ___ site drain

SITE PLANS--LANDSCAPING Continued

IN   OK

___ ___   PLANTING BEDS   02400
            ___ AGGREGATE   02400   (02495)
            ___ WOOD CHIP   02400   (02496)
            ___ dimensions ___ detail keys ___ notes/refs
            coord check: ___ paving ___ site drain

___ ___   WOOD CURBS OR BORDER BOARDS AT PLANTING BEDS   02500
            (02521/02522)
            ___ dimensions ___ detail keys ___ notes/refs
            coord check: ___ paving

___ ___   ROOT FEEDING PIPES   02480   (02490)
            ___ dimensions ___ detail keys ___ notes/refs
            coord check: ___ site drain

___ ___   LANDSCAPE IRRIGATION AND/OR SPRINKLER SYSTEM   02440
            (02441/02442)   (May be shown on separate Plumbing Plan.)
            ___ auto-timer
            ___ valves
            ___ hose bibbs and hydrants
            ___ sprinkler head locations
            coord check: ___ plumb ___ site drain

___ ___   DECORATIVE YARD LIGHTING AND TIMER SWITCH   16500   (16530)
            (May be shown on Electrical Drawings.)
            ___ locations ___ detail keys ___ notes/refs
            coord check: ___ elec

___ ___   LANDSCAPE MAINTENANCE STORAGE SHELTER   02440   (02499)
            ___ materials ___ dimensions ___ detail keys ___ notes/refs
            coord check: ___ plumb ___ elec

CHAPTER THREE--FLOOR PLANS AND INTERIOR ELEVATIONS   3.0 - 3.42

FLOOR PLANS AND INTERIOR ELEVATIONS--INTRODUCTION

The checklists in this chapter do double duty by covering interior
elevation components as well as floor plan items. One main point
about interior elevations: Those that mainly show fixtures and
equipment rather than major design features may not have to be drawn
at all. Consider using a fixture heights schedule that shows the
appearance and heights of all typical fixtures, and rely on the
floor plans to show their locations.

Floor plans are the start point and reference point for most other
drawings. Drawings such as elevations and consultants' plans are
derived directly from floor plans. Other drawings are derived indi-
rectly, as when a window detail is referenced from the window schedule
and the window schedule is derived from the floor plan. The final
point of reference is still the floor plan.

Checking and coordination problems arise when work is created or referenced in some sequence that bypasses or duplicates the plans. For
example, if door and window details are referenced directly from exterior elevations and also from the floor plans, there will be an unnecessary duplication of work and increased chance of error. ("Duplication leads to contradiction.")

Through all drafting, systems drafting, and checking processes, it's
imperative that all staff members work in reference to identical, up-
to-the-minute plan data. To assure this, all coordination checking
should be done using overlay transparencies whether the job is an
overlay drafting job or not.

ITEMS THAT SHOULD BE AVOIDED ON FLOOR PLAN DRAWINGS

____ The problem with floor plans is usually not so much one of over-
     drawing as one of crowded and uncoordinated drawing. Drafters
     tend to show too many separate layers or contracts on one sheet,
     especially in plans for smaller buildings. The alternative is to
     separate the layers of divergent data by using overlay drafting.
     Overlay makes it very convenient to sort out consultants' work,
     built-ins, equipment, special finishes, and other layers of infor-
     mation, and print them as separate sheets. That reduces crowding
     on any particular sheet, makes it easier to do checking, correc-
     tions and revisions, and it keeps all data in direct correlation
     to exactly the same original base sheet floor plan information.

____ Floor plan drawings, especially for smaller projects, tend to be
     oversized. 1/4" scale is common for residential work, for example,
     when far more complex institutional building floor plans are done
     quite adequately at 1/8" scale. The larger scales require more
     elaboration, more drawing, and hence, more time.

FLOOR PLANS AND INTERIOR ELEVATIONS--INTRODUCTION Continued

ITEMS THAT SHOULD BE AVOIDED ON FLOOR PLAN DRAWINGS Continued

____ Special rooms and spaces are sometimes segregated at larger scale for clarification. Apartment units, toilet rooms, commercial kitchens, and stair fire towers are frequently done this way. It's worth weighing the decision to duplicate these elements. They require considerable extra drafting, usually show no more or less than the smaller scale plans, and they're always a source of conflict as changes made on one scale drawing are not picked up on their counterpart. If you're using photoreduction/enlargement techniques, you can design special spaces at large scale and photoreduce them for smaller scale paste-ups. That cuts the duplicate drafting and helps assure consistency.

____ Notation is often redundant on floor plans. Any general condition can best be indicated in one general note of the type that says, for example: "All ceilings are 9'-0" high unless noted otherwise."

____ Textures, crosshatching, and materials indications are often overdone. Partial indications, such as a corner portion of tile pattern to show flooring, is faster and more readable than a complete grid of tile.

____ Wall construction is also frequently overdrawn. Wall construction can be shown either with partial materials indications at corners; a general "unless noted otherwise" note if it happens that most construction is of one type; graphic tape patterns; or with wall identification bubbles referenced to a wall section detail drawing or schedule.

____ Symbols can often be simpler than those commonly used. A simple "T" with detail and sheet number is faster to make and just as clear as the usual, more elaborate detail or section reference bubble.

____ Dimensions without feet and inch marks are just as clear as those with such marks, and elimination of the marks helps clean up drawings considerably. Dimension arrowheads made with simple dots or slashes are just as readable as more elaborate symbols. And notation leader lines really need no arrowheads at all.

COORDINATION

____ The key to all coordination derived from floor plans is the use of direct, one-to-one layering of base sheets and overlays. Overlay drafting, when managed and monitored according to the rules, guarantees 100% coordination between all consultants on the job.

FLOOR PLANS AND INTERIOR ELEVATIONS--INTRODUCTION Continued

COORDINATION Continued

____ Specific suggested coordination checks are referenced throughout
      the floor plan checklists.

ITEMS SUITED TO SYSTEMS DRAFTING, PASTE-UP, AND OVERLAY

____ Floor plans for working drawings can be recycled directly from the
      floor plans created during design development. When making the
      original floor plans, avoid showing data other than just plain bare
      linework. Do all rendering, alternate schemes, furniture, notes,
      and dimensions on overlays. That keeps the original plan clean
      and clear, ready for later direct reuse in working drawings. (By
      using this method, some firms are routinely 20% finished with work-
      ing drawings the day they start them.)

____ After final presentation drawings and approvals, architectural
      floor plans can be completed to a point of usability by the consult-
      ants--that is, with plumbing fixtures and drains for the plumbing
      drafters, equipment to be vented for HVAC work, door swings shown
      to aid the electrical engineer in switching of lights, etc. Then
      plans can be copied at direct one-to-one size on diazo sepia line
      polyester and distributed to all consultant and architectural draft-
      ing staff. The architectural staff will proceed with uniquely
      architectural information on their overlays (such as assembly and
      reference notes, and door, window, and finish schedule symbols),
      while consultants' drafters do their particular specialties on
      their overlays.

____ There's no better way to assure 100% coordination between all par-
      ticipants on the job than to have everyone working in reference
      to exactly the same base sheet information. Besides initial co-
      ordination, this method allows precise overlay comparisons of
      all work when checking for errors, omissions, and interferences.
      And at the conclusion of the job, it allows for screened shadow
      printing of background information in subdued contrast with solid-
      line overlay information. It's also an easy step from this point
      to go to multicolor offset printing--to maximize sharpness, dif-
      ferentiation, and clarity in the final printed documents.

____ Floor plans provide excellent opportunities for extensive use of
      tape, applique, and paste-up drafting. As soon as any basic scheme
      is established, identify all repetitive rooms or clusters of rooms.
      Hardline the repetitive units or rooms just once without redrawing
      them, and copy them in multiple for paste-up. Copies have to be ex-
      act one-to-one size reproductions. That requires contact printing
      on a vacuum frame. Produce other portions of the plan required for
      the paste-up, such as stairs, elevators, etc., and make direct one-
      to-one size contact prints of those portions to add to the paste-up.

FLOOR PLANS AND INTERIOR ELEVATIONS--INTRODUCTION Continued

ITEMS SUITED TO SYSTEMS DRAFTING, PASTE-UP, AND OVERLAY Continued

____ Tape drafting can be used for all walls and partitions. Tape goes
noticeably faster than hand drafting, but it takes several days to
get the speed up. A popular graphic tape is "ruby red litho" tape,
which comes in 1/16", 1/8", etc. widths. It's translucent to the
eye while being intensely opaque in printing processes. Ink drafting can augment the tape work and is useful for single lines and
small additions to wall tape linework.

____ Smaller repetitive elements on floor plans such as door swings,
fixtures, room names, north arrows, etc. can be pasted up from
small, clear film elements. Such elements can be made as intense
black toner copies on clear polyester by using office copiers, or
they can be sepia diazo film copies. Small- and medium-size elements like these are usually stored in slot boxes, envelopes, or
three-ring binder plastic pocket sheets like those used to store
35mm slides. They can be adhered with transparent tape, double-
sided tape, or "glu-stick" products. Since the object is to keep
the original floor plan itself free and clear of anything but pure
construction linework, the additional paste-up and applique items
are applied to architectural and engineering overlays.

____ The smallest repetitive elements such as switches, light fixtures,
diffusers, unit heaters, etc., are most convenient as dry transfer
rub-on appliques or pre-cut, thin film stickyback appliques. The
pre-cut stickybacks are preferable in most cases because they're
easy to apply, remove, or reposition.

FLOOR PLANS--GENERAL REFERENCE INFORMATION

IN   OK

___ ___   DRAWING TITLES AND SCALE

___ ___   ARROWS SHOWING COMPASS NORTH AND REFERENCE NORTH

___ ___   MODULAR GRID OR STRUCTURAL COLUMN GRID WITH NUMBER AND
            LETTER COORDINATES

___ ___   SQUARE FOOTAGE TOTALS:
            ___ building
            ___ auxiliary structures
            ___ decks and balconies
            ___ rooms (name or number)
            ___ exterior areas

___ ___   KEY PLAN

___ ___   INTERIOR ELEVATION ARROW SYMBOLS AND REFERENCE NUMBERS

___ ___   EXTERIOR ELEVATION ARROW SYMBOLS AND REFERENCE NUMBERS

___ ___   OVERALL CROSS SECTION LINES AND KEYS

___ ___   MATCH-UP LINE, OVERLAP LINE, AND REFERENCE IF FLOOR PLAN IS
            CONTINUED ON ANOTHER SHEET

___ ___   SPACE FOR ITEMS N.I.C.

___ ___   NOTE ON N.I.C. ITEMS TO BE INSTALLED, CONNECTED BY CONTRACTOR

___ ___   OUTLINE OF FUTURE BUILDING ADDITIONS

___ ___   REMODELING
            ___ existing work to remain as is
            ___ existing work to relocate
            ___ existing work to be removed
            ___ existing work to be repaired or altered

___ ___   GENERAL NOTES

___ ___   BUILDING CODE/FIRE CODE REFERENCES

___ ___   MATERIALS HATCHING OR POCHE

___ ___   DETAIL KEYS

___ ___   DRAWING CROSS REFERENCES

___ ___   SPECIFICATION REFERENCES

FLOOR PLANS--WALL DRAWING COMPONENTS

NOTE: Interior elevation components are to be identified from the
       floor plan checklists.

IN   OK

___ ___ OUTLINE AND NOTED HEIGHTS
         ___ low partitions
         ___ screens
         ___ prefab storage walls
         ___ dividers
         ___ planter walls
         ___ door and window openings

___ ___ OUTLINE OF CONSTRUCTED VENEERS
         ___ paneling
         ___ dados
         ___ wainscots

___ ___ BROKEN-LINE OUTLINES
         ___ overhangs
         ___ canopies
         ___ overhead balconies
         ___ coves
         ___ valances
         ___ other projections
         ___ wall lines at framed openings
         ___ thru-ceiling or upper floor openings
         ___ hatchways, access panels or scuttles

FLOOR PLANS--WALL DESIGN CONSIDERATIONS AND SPECIAL COMPONENTS

IN   OK

___ ___ PROTECTIVE RAILS, BUMPERS, OR CORNER GUARDS AT WALLS, GLAZ-
         ING, COLUMNS, OR DOOR JAMBS SUBJECT TO DAMAGE

___ ___ ANCHORS OR FRAMING CONNECTION FOR ALL WALL-MOUNTED FIXTURES
         AND EQUIPMENT

___ ___ WATERPROOFING AND CAULKING AT ALL WALLS AND OPENINGS EXPOSED
         TO MOISTURE

___ ___ THERMAL INSULATION AT ALL EXTERIOR WALLS

___ ___ WEATHERSTRIPPING AT ALL OPENINGS EXPOSED TO WEATHER

___ ___ EXTERIOR WALL OPENINGS
         ___ sill ___ opening sizes ___ detail keys ___ notes/refs
         coord check: ___ struct frame/lintels ___ ext elev

FLOOR PLANS--EXTERIOR WALL CONSTRUCTION

IN   OK

___ ___   EXTERIOR WALLS

    ___   ADOBE   04200   (04212)

    ___   BRICK   04200   (04210)

    ___   BRICK CAVITY WALL   04200   (04214)

    ___   BRICK VENEER   04200   (04215)

    ___   CONCRETE BLOCK, REINFORCED   04200   (04230)

    ___   CONCRETE, CAST-IN-PLACE   03300   (03316)

    ___   CONCRETE, PRECAST   03400   (03450)

    ___   CONCRETE, PRECAST PANELS   03400   (03411)

    ___   CONCRETE, TILT-UP   03400   (03430)

    ___   GLAZED CURTAIN WALLS   08900   (08900)

    ___   METAL SIDING   07400   (07411)

    ___   STONE   04400   (04400)

    ___   CUT STONE   04400   (04420)

    ___   FLAGSTONE   04400   (04440)

    ___   MARBLE VENEER   04400   (04451)

    ___   NATURAL STONE VENEER   04400   (04450)

    ___   ROUGH STONE   04400   (04410)

    ___   STUCCO   09230   (09230)

    ___   WOOD FRAMING AND SHEATHING   06100   (06110)

    ___   WOOD SIDING   07400   (07461)

    ___ materials ___ dimensions ___ detail keys ___ notes/refs
coord check: ___ struct footings/frame ___ roof drain
    ___ ext elev ___ ref clg

FLOOR PLANS--COLUMN AND POST CONSTRUCTION

IN   OK

___ ___   COLUMNS AND POSTS

___   REINFORCED BRICK 04200 (04216)

___   CONCRETE 03300 (03317)

___   REINFORCED CONCRETE BLOCK 04200 (04230)

___   STEEL WF 05100 (05110)

___   TUBULAR STEEL 05100 (05123)

___   WOOD 06100 (06101/06102)

___ materials ___ dimensions ___ detail keys ___ notes/refs
coord check: ___ struct footings/frame ___ roof drain
___ ext elev ___ ref clg

___ ___   FIREPROOFING AT COLUMNS AND POSTS 07250 (07250)
___ materials ___ locations ___ detail keys ___ notes/refs
coord check: ___ code ___ int elev ___ fin sched

___ ___   COLUMN AND POST CORNER GUARDS 10260 (10260)
___ materials ___ locations ___ detail keys ___ notes/refs
coord check: ___ wall anch ___ int elev

FLOOR PLANS--INTERIOR BEARING WALL CONSTRUCTION

IN   OK

___ ___   INTERIOR BEARING WALLS

          ___   BRICK   04200   (04210)

          ___   CONCRETE BLOCK   04200   (04220)

          ___   CONCRETE, CAST-IN-PLACE   03300   (03316)

          ___   CONCRETE, PRECAST PANELS   03300   (03411)

          ___   METAL STUD FRAMING   05400   (05410)

          ___   STONE   04400   (04400)

          ___   WOOD STUD FRAMING   06100   (06110)

          ___ materials ___ dimensions ___ detail keys ___ notes/refs
          coord check: ___ struct footings/frame ___ int elev
              ___ ref clg ___ roof drain ___ fin sched

___ ___   FIREPROOFING   07250   (07250)
          ___ materials ___ dimensions ___ detail keys ___ notes/refs
          coord check: ___ code ___ int elev ___ fin sched

___ ___   CORNER GUARDS   10260   (10260)
          ___ materials ___ locations ___ detail keys ___ notes/refs
          coord check: ___ wall anch ___ int elev

FLOOR PLANS--INTERIOR PARTITION CONSTRUCTION

IN   OK

____ ____   INTERIOR PARTITIONS
             ____ BRICK   04200   (04210)
             ____ BRICK VENEER   04200   (04215)
             ____ CONCRETE BLOCK   04200   (04220)
             ____ GLASS UNIT MASONRY   04200   (04270)
             ____ STONE   04400   (04400)
             ____ CUT STONE   04400   (04420)
             ____ MARBLE VENEER   04400   (04451)
             ____ NATURAL STONE VENEER   04400   (04450)
             ____ WOOD FRAMING AND SHEATHING   06100   (06110)
             ____ WIRE MESH PARTITIONS   10600   (10601)
             ____ WOOD PANELING   06400   (06420)
             ____ GYPSUM LATH AND PLASTER   09200   (09202)
             ____ METAL LATH AND PLASTER   09200   (09203)
             ____ GYPSUM WALLBOARD   09250   (09250)
             ____ materials ____ dimensions ____ detail keys ____ notes/refs
             coord check: ____ floor anch ____ ref clg ____ int elev
                     ____ fin sched ____ elec

____ ____   GLAZED WALLS
             (Fixed glass provided with removable stops on one side.
             For other components and assemblies, see Windows.)
             ____ OBSCURE GLASS/ROUGH AND FIGURED   08800   (08815)
             ____ WIRE GLASS   08800   (08814)
             ____ PLASTIC   08800   (08840)
             ____ LAMINATED SAFETY GLASS   08800   (08822)
             ____ INSULATING GLASS   08800   (08823)
             ____ STAINED GLASS   12100   (12170)
             ____ TEMPERED GLASS   08800   (08813)
             ____ MIRROR GLASS   08800   (08830)
             ____ TWO-WAY SURVEILLANCE MIRRORS   08800   (08835)
             ____ materials ____ dimensions ____ detail keys ____ notes/refs
             coord check: ____ int elev ____ ref clg ____ frame sched
                     ____ fin sched

____ ____   MOVABLE WALLS   10600   (10615)
             ____ materials ____ dimensions ____ detail keys ____ notes/refs
             coord check: ____ struct frame ____ int elev ____ ref clg
                     ____ fin sched

____ ____   DEMOUNTABLE PARTITIONS   10600   (10610)
             ____ materials ____ dimensions ____ detail keys ____ notes/refs
             coord check: ____ struct frame ____ int elev ____ ref clg
                     ____ fin sched

____ ____   FOLDING PARTITIONS   10600   (10620)
             ____ materials ____ dimensions ____ detail keys ____ notes/refs
             coord check: ____ struct frame ____ int elev ____ ref clg
                     ____ fin sched

FLOOR PLANS--SPECIAL WALL CONSTRUCTION: FURRING, CHASES, ETC.

IN   OK

___ ___ FURRED WALLS
         ___ materials ___ dimensions ___ detail keys ___ notes/refs
         coord check: ___ struct ___ int/ext elev ___ ref clg
               ___ plumb ___ hvac ___ elec

___ ___ ELECTRIC CLOSETS AND PANELBOARDS 16050 (16160)
         ___ dimensions ___ detail keys ___ notes/refs
         coord check: ___ elec ___ plumb/mech chases ___ int elev

___ ___ ELECTRICAL RACEWAYS AND CHASES 16050 (16110)
         ___ dimensions ___ detail keys ___ notes/refs
         coord check: ___ elec ___ struct frame ___ plumb ___ hvac

___ ___ TELEPHONE SWITCHING CLOSETS AND PANELBOARDS 16700 (16740)
         ___ dimensions ___ detail keys ___ notes/refs
         coord check: ___ elec ___ elec/mech chases ___ int elev

___ ___ TELEPHONE WIRING CHASES 16700 (16740)
         ___ dimensions ___ detail keys ___ notes/refs
         coord check: ___ struct frame ___ plumb ___ hvac ___ elec

___ ___ VERTICAL CHUTES IN WALLS 14500 (14560)
         ___ materials ___ dimensions ___ detail keys ___ notes/refs
         coord check: ___ struct frame ___ hvac ___ elec chases
               ___ int elev ___ cross sect ___ roof

___ ___ PNEUMATIC TUBES 14500 (14581)
         ___ locations ___ detail keys ___ notes/refs
         coord check: ___ struct frame ___ plumb chases ___ hvac
               ___ elec

___ ___ THRU-WALL SLEEVES
         ___ materials ___ dimensions ___ detail keys ___ notes/refs
         coord check: ___ struct frame ___ int/ext elev ___ plumb
               ___ hvac ___ elec

___ ___ VENT CHASES 15600
         ___ dimensions ___ detail keys ___ notes/refs
         coord check: ___ struct frame ___ ref clg ___ roof
               ___ cross sect ___ plumb ___ hvac ___ elec chases

___ ___ PLUMBING CHASES 15400
         ___ dimensions ___ detail keys ___ notes/refs
         coord check: ___ plumb ___ struct frame ___ ref clg
               ___ roof ___ cross sect ___ hvac ___ elec chases

___ ___ PLUMBING CLEANOUT ACCESS COVERS 15400 (15423)
         ___ locations ___ detail keys ___ notes/refs
         coord check: ___ plumb ___ wall anch ___ int elev

FLOOR PLANS--SPECIAL WALL CONSTRUCTION: FURRING, CHASES, ETC. Cont.

IN   OK

___ ___ PLUMBING CHASE ACCESS DOORS 08300/10250 (08305/10250)
          ___ materials ___ dimensions ___ detail keys ___ notes/refs
          coord check: ___ plumb ___ int elev ___ door sched

___ ___ ACCESS PANELS 08300/10220/10240 (08305/10222/10245)
          ___ materials ___ dimensions ___ detail keys ___ notes/refs
          coord check: ___ wall anch ___ int/ext elev

___ ___ GRILLES 10240 (10240)
          ___ materials ___ dimensions ___ detail keys ___ notes/refs
          coord check: ___ wall anch ___ int/ext elev

___ ___ IN-WALL ROOF DRAINS 15400 (15406)
          ___ materials ___ dimensions ___ detail keys ___ notes/refs
          coord check: ___ plumb ___ struct frame ___ roof
          ___ cross sect

___ ___ HEAVY FLOOR OR WALL-MOUNTED EQUIPMENT THAT MAY REQUIRE SPECIAL
          STRUCTURAL SUPPORT
          ___ materials ___ dimensions ___ detail keys ___ notes/refs
          coord check: ___ struct frame ___ slab/floor ___ wall anch
          ___ int elev

___ ___ WALL SAFES 11020 (11028)
          ___ materials ___ dimensions ___ detail keys ___ notes/refs
          coord check: ___ wall frame ___ elec/alarm ___ int elev

___ ___ VAULTS 11020/13140 (11021/13140)
          ___ materials ___ dimensions ___ detail keys ___ notes/refs
          coord check: ___ wall/floor frame ___ elec/alarm ___ int elev

FLOOR PLANS--ACOUSTICAL TREATMENTS AND NOISE CONTROL

IN   OK

___ ___ NOISE BARRIER CONSTRUCTION WHERE CONVECTORS PASS THROUGH
         PARTITIONS 13080 (13080)
         ___ materials ___ dimensions ___ detail keys ___ notes/refs
         coord check: ___ hvac

___ ___ VIBRATION AND NOISE CONTROL AT WALL-MOUNTED TVS, INTERCOMS,
         FANS, AND OTHER MOVING OR NOISE-MAKING EQUIPMENT 13080 (13080)
         ___ materials ___ dimensions ___ detail keys ___ notes/refs
         coord check: ___ wall anch ___ elec ___ hvac

___ ___ VIBRATION AND NOISE CONTROL AT MECHANICAL EQUIPMENT 15200
         (15200)
         ___ materials ___ dimensions ___ detail keys ___ notes/refs
         coord check: ___ hvac

___ ___ SOUND ISOLATION WALLS 09500/13080 (09530/13080)
         ___ materials ___ dimensions ___ detail keys ___ notes/refs
         coord check: ___ ref clg

___ ___ ACOUSTICAL PLASTER 09500 (09520)
         ___ dimensions ___ detail keys ___ notes/refs
         coord check: ___ int elev ___ fin sched

___ ___ ACOUSTICAL WALL PANELS 09500 (09511)
         ___ materials ___ dimensions ___ detail keys ___ notes/refs
         coord check: ___ wall anch ___ int elev ___ fin sched

___ ___ ACOUSTICAL WALL TILES 09500 (09512)
         ___ materials ___ dimensions ___ detail keys ___ notes/refs
         coord check: ___ int elev ___ fin sched

___ ___ ACOUSTICAL INSULATION 09500 (09530)
         ___ materials ___ dimensions ___ detail keys ___ notes/refs
         coord check: ___ int elev ___ ref clg ___ wall sect
         ___ fin sched

FLOOR PLANS--WATERPROOFING, SHIELDING, AND INSULATION

IN   OK

___ ___   WALLS WITH MEMBRANE WATERPROOFING 07100 (07110)
          ___ waterproof barriers behind drinking fountains and sinks
          ___ materials ___ dimensions ___ detail keys ___ notes/refs
          coord check: ___ floor ___ wall sect ___ plumb

___ ___   ELECTROMAGNETIC SHIELDING 16600 (16650)
          ___ materials ___ dimensions ___ detail keys ___ notes/refs
          coord check: ___ floor/clg ___ wall sect ___ elec

___ ___   RADIATION SHIELDING 13090 (13090)
          ___ materials ___ dimensions ___ detail keys ___ notes/refs
          coord check: ___ struct/frame ___ floor/clg ___ wall sect
          ___ elec

___ ___   BATT THERMAL INSULATION 07200 (07213)
          ___ dimensions ___ detail keys ___ notes/refs
          coord check: ___ wall sect ___ clg/roof ___ hvac

___ ___   RIGID INSULATION 07200 (07212)
          ___ dimensions ___ detail keys ___ notes/refs
          coord check: ___ wall sect ___ clg/roof ___ hvac

___ ___   GRANULAR INSULATION 07200 (07216)
          ___ dimensions ___ detail keys ___ notes/refs
          coord check: ___ wall sect ___ hvac

FLOOR PLANS--WALL-MOUNTED ITEMS

IN   OK

___ ___   WALL-MOUNTED ACCESSORIES AND FIXTURES

           ___ MIRRORS 08800/10800 (08830/10810)

           ___ PEGBOARDS 06400 (06423)

           ___ CHALKBOARDS 10100 (10110)

           ___ TACKBOARDS 10100 (10120)

           ___ PICTURE RAILS 05500/06400 (05509/06445)

           ___ MAP RAILS 05500/06400 (05509/06446)

           ___ PROJECTION SCREENS 11130 (11131)

           ___ HOOKS/HANGERS 05500 (05507/05508)

           ___ SIGNS 10400 (10440)

           ___ locations/heights ___ detail keys ___ notes/refs
           coord check: ___ int elev ___ wall frame/anch

___ ___   FIRE EXTINGUISHER CABINETS 10520 (10522)
           ___ locations/heights ___ detail keys ___ notes/refs
           coord check: ___ code ___ plumb ___ wall anch ___ int elev

___ ___   FIRE HOSE CABINETS 15500 (15532)
           ___ locations/heights ___ detail keys ___ notes/refs
           coord check: ___ code ___ plumb ___ wall anch ___ int elev

___ ___   DRINKING FOUNTAINS 15400 (15461)
           ___ water protection at wall behind drinking fountain
           ___ locations/heights ___ detail keys ___ notes/refs
           coord check: ___ plumb ___ wall anch ___ int elev

FLOOR PLANS--WALL-MOUNTED ITEMS, ELECTRICAL

IN   OK

___ ___ WALL-MOUNTED ELECTRICAL AND COMMUNICATIONS FIXTURES

       ___ CLOCKS 16700 (16730)

       ___ LAMPS 16500 (16501)

       ___ BURGLAR DETECTORS 16700 (16720)

       ___ BURGLAR ALARMS 16700 (16727)

       ___ SPEAKERS 16700 (16770)

       ___ ANNUNCIATORS 16700 (16770)

       ___ THERMOSTATS 15931 (15931)

       ___ CLOSED-CIRCUIT TV MONITORS 16700 (16780)

       ___ SURVEILLANCE TV CAMERAS 16700 (16780)

       ___ locations/heights ___ detail keys ___ notes/refs
coord check: ___ elec ___ int elev ___ wall anch

___ ___ WALL-MOUNTED FIRE ALARMS

       ___ SMOKE DETECTORS 16720 (16725)

       ___ FIRE DETECTORS 16720 (16721)

       ___ FIRE ALARMS 16720 (16721)

       ___ locations/heights ___ detail keys ___ notes/refs
coord check: ___ code ___ elec ___ int elev ___ wall anch

___ ___ FIRE EXIT SIGNS 10400 (10455)
       ___ locations/heights ___ detail keys ___ notes/refs
coord check: ___ code ___ elec ___ int elev ___ wall anch

FLOOR PLANS--HVAC EQUIPMENT AND FIXTURES AT WALLS

IN   OK

___ ___   METAL HEATING/COOLING UNIT ENCLOSURES   05500   (05551)
    ___ dimensions ___ detail keys ___ notes/refs
    coord check: ___ hvac ___ plumb ___ elec ___ int elev

___ ___   UNIT VENTILATORS 15700/16850   (15762/16850)
    ___ locations ___ detail keys ___ notes/refs
    coord check: ___ hvac ___ elec ___ ref clg ___ int elev

___ ___   UNIT HEATERS 15700/16850   (15700/16850)
    ___ locations ___ detail keys ___ notes/refs
    coord check: ___ hvac ___ elec ___ int elev

___ ___   CONVECTORS AND ENCLOSURES 15700/16850   (15700/16850)
    ___ locations ___ detail keys ___ notes/refs
    coord check: ___ hvac ___ plumb ___ elec ___ int elev

___ ___   REGISTERS 15800   (15870)
    ___ locations ___ detail keys ___ notes/refs
    coord check: ___ hvac ___ wall anch ___ int elev

___ ___   DIFFUSERS 15800   (15870)
    ___ locations ___ detail keys ___ notes/refs
    coord check: ___ hvac ___ wall anch ___ int elev

FLOOR PLANS--SHELVING, CABINETS, AND COUNTERTOPS

IN   OK

___ ___   WALL-MOUNTED SHELVES
            ___ WOOD SHELVING 06400 (06412)
            ___ METAL STORAGE SHELVING 10670 (10671)
            ___ WIRE SHELVING 10670 (10673)
            ___ materials ___ dimensions ___ detail keys ___ notes/refs
            coord check: ___ wall anch ___ furn ___ int elev

___ ___   WALL-MOUNTED CABINETS
            ___ WOOD CABINETS 06400 (06410)
            ___ WOOD CASEWORK 12300 (12302)
            ___ METAL CASEWORK 12300 (12301)
            ___ materials ___ dimensions ___ detail keys ___ notes/refs
            coord check: ___ wall anch ___ furn ___ int elev
                 ___ ref clg/soffit ___ elec

___ ___   WALL-MOUNTED WOOD SHELF COUNTERTOPS 06400 (06412)
            ___ materials ___ dimensions ___ detail keys ___ notes/refs
            coord check: ___ wall anch ___ furn ___ int elev ___ elec

___ ___   WOOD BASE CABINET COUNTERTOPS 06400 (06414)
            ___ materials ___ dimensions ___ detail keys ___ notes/refs
            coord check: ___ wall anch ___ furn ___ int elev ___ elec

___ ___   TILE COUNTERTOPS 09300 (09318)
            ___ materials ___ dimensions ___ detail keys ___ notes/refs
            coord check: ___ wall anch ___ furn ___ int elev ___ elec

___ ___   METAL COUNTERTOPS 11400/12300 (11400/12300)
            ___ materials ___ dimensions ___ detail keys ___ notes/refs
            coord check: ___ wall anch ___ furn ___ int elev ___ elec

___ ___   STONE COUNTERTOPS 04400 (04420)
            ___ materials ___ dimensions ___ detail keys ___ notes/refs
            coord check: ___ wall anch ___ furn ___ int elev ___ elec

___ ___   PLASTIC FINISH COUNTERTOPS 06200 (06240)
            ___ materials ___ dimensions ___ detail keys ___ notes/refs
            coord check: ___ wall anch ___ furn ___ int elev ___ elec

___ ___   UNIT KITCHEN CABINETS 11450 (11460)
            ___ materials ___ dimensions ___ detail keys ___ notes/refs
            coord check: ___ wall anch ___ furn ___ int elev ___ plumb
                 ___ vent ___ elec

FLOOR PLANS--SHELVING, CABINETS, AND COUNTERTOPS Continued

IN   OK

___ ___   WORKBENCHES
           ___ WOOD 06400 (06453)
           ___ INDUSTRIAL 11500 (11511)
           ___ materials ___ dimensions ___ detail keys ___ notes/refs
           coord check: ___ wall anch ___ furn ___ int elev ___ plumb
                    ___ vent ___ elec

___ ___   LOCKERS 10500 (10500)
           ___ soffit
           ___ locker base or pedestal
           ___ materials ___ dimensions ___ detail keys ___ notes/refs
           coord check: ___ wall anch ___ slab/floor ___ int elev
                    ___ ref clg/soffit

FLOOR PLANS--WALL-MOUNTED ART AND PLAQUES

IN   OK

___ ___   WALL-MOUNTED MURALS 12100 (12110)
          ___ materials ___ dimensions ___ detail keys ___ notes/refs
          coord check: ___ wall anch ___ int/ext elev

___ ___   BAS-RELIEF 12100 (12150)
          ___ materials ___ dimensions ___ detail keys ___ notes/refs
          coord check: ___ wall anch ___ int/ext elev

___ ___   SCULPTURE/STATUARY 12100 (12140)
          ___ materials ___ dimensions ___ detail keys ___ notes/refs
          coord check: ___ struct frame/slab ___ wall anch
          ___ int/ext elev

___ ___   CORNERSTONE PLAQUE 10400 (10420)
          ___ location ___ detail keys ___ notes/refs
          coord check: ___ wall anch ___ ext elev

___ ___   ARCHITECT'S PLAQUE 10400 (10420)
          ___ location ___ detail keys ___ notes/refs
          coord check: ___ wall anch ___ ext elev

FLOOR PLANS--WINDOWS, DESIGN CONSIDERATIONS AND DRAWING COMPONENTS

IN   OK

____ ____ WINDOW OPENINGS DESIGNED AND LOCATED TO AVOID CONFLICT OF TRIM, MOLDING, SILLS, OR STOOLS WITH ADJACENT WALLS, WINDOWS, OR DOORS

____ ____ SPANDREL GLASS INTEGRATED WITH FENESTRATION

____ ____ GLASS LINES

____ ____ SILL AND STOOL LINES

____ ____ METAL FRAME SCHEDULE

____ ____ OPERABLE DIRECTIONS

    ____ horizontal sliding windows

    ____ swings for vertical casements

    ____ pivot windows

    ____ awning windows

____ ____ WINDOW SYMBOLS KEYED TO WINDOW SCHEDULE

____ ____ GLAZING TYPES

    ____ PLATE/FLOAT 08800 (08811)

    ____ DOUBLE GLAZING 08800 (08802)

    ____ SPANDREL GLASS 08800 (08817)

    ____ OBSCURE GLASS/ROUGH AND FIGURED 08800 (08815)

    ____ WIRE GLASS 08800 (08814)

    ____ PLASTIC 08600 (08620)

    ____ PLASTIC INSULATING 08800 (08845)

    ____ LAMINATED SAFETY GLASS 08800 (08822)

    ____ INSULATING GLASS 08800 (08802/08823)

    ____ STAINED GLASS 12100 (12170)

    ____ TEMPERED GLASS 08800 (08813)

    coord check: ____ ext elev ____ window sched

FLOOR PLANS--WINDOW TYPES

IN   OK

___ ___   WINDOW TYPES

___   GLAZED CURTAIN WALLS 08900 (08910)

___   STEEL WINDOWS 08500 (08510)

___   AWNING 08500 (08511)

___   CASEMENT 08500 (08512)

___   JALOUSIE 08500 (08514)

___   PIVOTED 08500 (08515)

___   ALUMINUM WINDOWS 08500 (08520)

___   AWNING 08500 (08521)

___   CASEMENT 08500 (08522)

___   DOUBLE HUNG 08500 (08523)

___   JALOUSIE 08500 (08527)

___   PIVOTED 08500 (08525)

___   SLIDING 08500 (08527)

___   WOOD WINDOWS 08600 (08610)

___   AWNING 08600 (08611)

___   CASEMENT 08600 (08612)

___   DOUBLE HUNG 08600 (08613)

___   PIVOTED 08600 (08615)

___   SLIDING 08600 (08617)

___ locations/sizes ___ detail keys ___ notes/refs
coord check: ___ ext elev ___ window sched ___ wall anch
___ struct frame/lintels

___ ___   INTEGRATED STOREFRONT SYSTEM 08400 (08400)
___ materials ___ dimensions ___ detail keys ___ notes/refs
coord check: ___ frame sched ___ wall anch ___ ext elev
___ wall sect ___ struct frame/lintels

FLOOR PLANS--WINDOWS, WINDOW ACCESSORIES, AND RELATED CONSTRUCTION

IN   OK

___ ___   STOREFRONT AND CURTAIN WALL MULLIONS 08400/08900
          ___ materials ___ dimensions ___ detail keys ___ notes/refs
          coord check: ___ frame sched ___ wall anch ___ window sched
               ___ ext elev ___ wall sect ___ struct frame/lintels

___ ___   EXTERIOR SHUTTERS
          ___ METAL 10240 (10245)
          ___ WOOD 06200 (06235)
          ___ materials ___ dimensions ___ detail keys ___ notes/refs
          coord check: ___ code ___ wall anch ___ ext elev

___ ___   PROTECTIVE GRILLES AT WINDOWS ACCESSIBLE TO PUBLIC WALKWAYS,
          EXTERIOR STAIRS, OR FIRE ESCAPES 10240 (10241)
          ___ fixed ___ operable
          ___ materials ___ dimensions ___ detail keys ___ notes/refs
          coord check: ___ code ___ wall anch ___ ext elev

___ ___   WIRE MESH WINDOW GUARDS 10240 (10242)
          ___ fixed ___ operable
          ___ materials ___ dimensions ___ detail keys ___ notes/refs
          coord check: ___ code ___ wall anch ___ ext elev

___ ___   SECURITY WINDOWS 08650 (08651)
          ___ materials ___ dimensions ___ detail keys ___ notes/refs
          coord check: ___ code ___ wall anch ___ ext elev

___ ___   WINDOW BURGLAR ALARMS 16700 (16727)
          ___ locations ___ detail keys ___ notes/refs
          coord check: ___ wall anch ___ elec

___ ___   WINDOW CLEANER'S HOOKS 05500 (05507)
          ___ locations ___ detail keys ___ notes/refs
          coord check: ___ code ___ wall anch ___ roof

___ ___   INTERIOR DRAPE, BLIND, OR WINDOW SHADE TRACKS 12500 (12502)
          ___ materials ___ dimensions ___ detail keys ___ notes/refs
          coord check: ___ furn ___ solar ___ hardwr sched
               ___ int elev ___ hvac

___ ___   INTERIOR SHUTTERS 12500 (12527)
          ___ materials ___ dimensions ___ detail keys ___ notes/refs
          coord check: ___ code ___ wall anch ___ hardwr sched
               ___ int elev

FLOOR PLANS--DOORS, DESIGN CONSIDERATIONS

IN   OK

___ ___ VARIETY OF DOOR SIZES KEPT TO MINIMUM TO SIMPLIFY DOOR SCHEDULES
          AND CONSTRUCTION

___ ___ DOORS AVOIDED AT HEAVY TRAFFIC AREAS UNLESS ABSOLUTELY NECESSARY

___ ___ REMOVABLE WINTER AIR LOCK STORM DOORS AT ENTRY VESTIBULES

___ ___ REMOVABLE AND LOCKABLE STILES FOR EXTERIOR DOUBLE DOORS

___ ___ STRIKE SIDE OF DOORS LOCATED GENEROUS DISTANCE FROM POSTS,
          WING WALLS, WINDOW MULLIONS, OR OTHER VULNERABLE CONSTRUCTION

___ ___ DOOR JAMBS DESIGNED AND LOCATED TO AVOID CONFLICT OF MOLD-
          INGS OR TRIM THAT INTERSECT ADJACENT WALLS, DOORS, OR WINDOWS

___ ___ PROTECTIVE METAL JACKETS FOR DOOR OPENINGS SUBJECT TO DAMAGE

___ ___ DOOR OPENINGS LOCATED SO THAT DOORS AVOID TANGLING WITH
          NEIGHBORING DOORS IN ADJACENT WALLS

___ ___ DOORS OPENING ON OPPOSITE SIDES OF COMMON CORRIDOR STAGGERED
          WHERE VISUAL AND SOUND PRIVACY IS IMPORTANT

___ ___ DOORS OPENING TO TOILET ROOMS, DRESSING ROOMS, OTHER PRIVATE
          AREAS LOCATED AND HINGED TO BLOCK DIRECT VIEW INTO ROOMS
          (Avoid doors and use visual and acoustic screening instead of
          doors in heavily trafficked areas.)

___ ___ SOUNDPROOFING AND STRIPPING AT THRESHOLDS OF NOISY ROOMS

___ ___ WEATHERSTRIPPING AT PLENUM SPACE ACCESS DOORS

FLOOR PLANS--DOORS, DRAWING COMPONENTS

IN   OK

___ ___ DOOR OPENINGS
        ___ door swing or sliding direction
        ___ symbol key references to door schedule
        ___ thresholds
        ___ veneer notes

        ___ DIRECTION OF MOVEMENT
            ___ side sliding
            ___ split action/dutch door
            ___ folding
            ___ bifolding
            ___ pivoted
            ___ double-acting
            ___ vertical coil
            ___ vertical slide
            ___ center parting
coord check: ___ elec/switch   ___ hvac

___ ___ DOOR MATERIALS/CONSTRUCTION

        ___ STEEL 08100 (08110)

        ___ CUSTOM STEEL 08100 (08112)

        ___ PACKAGED STEEL 08100 (08115)

        ___ ALUMINUM 08100 (08120)

        ___ STAINLESS STEEL 08100 (08130)

        ___ BRONZE 08100 (08140)

        ___ FLUSH WOOD 08200 (08210)

        ___ WOOD PANEL 08200 (08212)

        ___ PLASTIC-FACED WOOD 08200 (08213)

        ___ STEEL-FACED WOOD 08200 (08214)

        ___ PLASTIC 08200 (08220)

        ___ KALAMEIN (metal clad) 08300 (08320)

        ___ WIRE MESH 10600 (10601)
        ___ materials ___ dimensions ___ detail keys ___ notes/refs
coord check: ___ ext elev ___ int elev ___ door sched
             ___ frame sched ___ hardwr sched

FLOOR PLANS--DOOR TYPES, ACCESSORIES, AND RELATED CONSTRUCTION

IN   OK

___ ___ DOOR TYPES

     ___ ACCORDION 08300   (08353)

     ___ AIR DOORS 15800   (15870)

     ___ AUTOMATIC 08400   (08425)

     ___ BLAST RESISTANT 08300   (08315)

     ___ COILING DOORS 08300   (08330 to 08332)

     ___ COILING GRILLES 08300   (08340 to 08342)

     ___ ELEVATOR DOORS 14200   (14200)

     ___ FLEXIBLE 08300   (08355)

     ___ FOLDING DOORS 08300   (08350)

     ___ PANEL FOLDING 08300   (08351)

     ___ METAL-CLAD 08300   (08320)

     ___ OVERHEAD 08300   (08360)

     ___ REVOLVING 08400   (08450)

     ___ SECTIONAL OVERHEAD 08300   (08361 to 08363)

     ___ SCREEN 08300   (08390)

     ___ SECURITY 08300   (08316)

     ___ SLIDING GLASS 08300   (08370)

     ___ SOUND RETARDANT 08300   (08380)

     ___ STOREFRONT ENTRY 08400   (08420)

     ___ STORM 08300   (08391)

     ___ opening sizes ___ detail keys ___ notes/refs
coord check: ___ ext elev ___ int elev ___ door sched
     ___ frame sched ___ hardwr sched ___ elec/switch

FLOOR PLANS--DOOR TYPES, ACCESSORIES, AND RELATED CONSTRUCTION   Cont.

IN   OK

___ ___   FIRE-RATED DOORS 08100 (08100)
           ___ automatic closing fire doors
           ___ opening sizes ___ detail keys ___ notes/refs
           coord check: ___ code ___ int elev ___ door sched
                ___ frame sched ___ hardwr sched ___ elec/switch

___ ___   SLIDING FIRE DOORS 08300 (08310)
           ___ opening sizes ___ detail keys ___ notes/refs
           coord check: ___ code ___ int elev ___ door sched
                ___ frame sched ___ hardwr sched ___ elec

___ ___   DOOR HEADERS OR LINTELS
           ___ materials ___ sizes ___ detail keys ___ notes/refs
           coord check: ___ struct frame/lintel

___ ___   JAMBS, FRAMES, AND DOOR BUCKS
           (Usually referenced and detailed keyed in the door schedule
           or door frame schedule. May be referenced and keyed on floor
           plans for smaller buildings.)
           ___ STANDARD STEEL FRAMES 08100 (08111)
           ___ CUSTOM STEEL FRAMES 08100 (08113)
           ___ PACKAGED STEEL DOORS AND FRAMES 08100 (08115)
           ___ WOOD 06100/06400 (06100/06400)
           ___ ALUMINUM STORE FRONT ENTRANCES 08400 (08410)
           ___ materials ___ sizes ___ detail keys ___ notes/refs
           coord check: ___ ext elev ___ int elev ___ door sched
                ___ frame sched ___ hardwr sched

___ ___   DOOR SADDLES OR SILLS 08700 (08740)
           ___ materials ___ detail keys ___ notes/refs
           coord check: ___ slab/floor anch ___ hardwr sched

___ ___   THRESHOLDS @ EXTERIOR DOORS 08700 (08740)
           ___ materials ___ dimensions ___ detail keys ___ notes/refs
           coord check: ___ slab/floor anch ___ hardwr sched

___ ___   ALARMS AT RESTRICTED EXIT DOORS 16700 (16728)
           ___ locations ___ notes/refs
           coord check: ___ code ___ door sched ___ elec

___ ___   WARNING SIGNS AT RESTRICTED EXIT DOORS 10400 (10440)
           ___ locations ___ notes/refs
           coord check: ___ code ___ int elev ___ door sched

FLOOR PLANS--DOOR TYPES, ACCESSORIES, AND RELATED CONSTRUCTION Cont.

IN   OK

___ ___   DOOR SIDE LIGHTS 08800 (08800)
          ___ detail keys ___ notes/refs
          coord check: ___ code ___ int elev ___ door sched

___ ___   FIXED MATCHING PANELS ABOVE WOOD FLUSH DOOR 06400 (06420)
          ___ materials ___ sizes ___ detail keys ___ notes/refs
          coord check: ___ int elev ___ ref clg ___ door sched
              ___ fin sched

___ ___   INVISIBLE DOORS IN PANELING 06400 (06420)
          ___ materials ___ sizes ___ detail keys ___ notes/refs
          coord check: ___ int elev ___ door sched ___ fin sched

___ ___   FLOOR-MOUNTED TRACKS FOR FOLDING DOORS 08700 (08745)
          ___ materials ___ dimensions ___ detail keys ___ notes/refs
          coord check: ___ slab/floor anch ___ wall anch ___ door sched
              ___ hardwr sched

___ ___   FLOOR-MOUNTED TRACKS FOR SLIDING DOORS 08700 (08746)
          ___ materials ___ dimensions ___ detail keys ___ notes/refs
          coord check: ___ slab/floor anch ___ wall anch ___ door sched
              ___ hardwr sched

___ ___   OVERHEAD TRACKS FOR FOLDING DOORS 08700 (08747)
          ___ materials ___ dimensions ___ detail keys ___ notes/refs
          coord check: ___ struct ___ ref clg ___ door sched
              ___ hardwr sched

___ ___   OVERHEAD TRACKS FOR SLIDING DOORS 08700 (08748)
          ___ materials ___ dimensions ___ detail keys ___ notes/refs
          coord check: ___ struct ___ ref clg ___ door sched
              ___ hardwr sched

___ ___   SLIDING METAL FIRE DOORS 08300 (08310)
          (Type of door operation, single slide or center-parting,
          inclined track or level track, manual or power-operated.)
          ___ single slide ___ center-parting ___ inclined/level track
          ___ manual operated ___ power operated
          ___ materials ___ dimensions ___ detail keys ___ notes/refs
          coord check: ___ code ___ struct ___ ref clg ___ door sched
              ___ elec

___ ___   AUTOMATIC DOOR ACTIVATING EQUIPMENT 08700 (08721)
          ___ location ___ detail keys ___ notes/refs
          coord check: ___ slab/floor ___ ref clg ___ door sched
              ___ elec

FLOOR PLANS--DOOR TYPES, ACCESSORIES, AND RELATED CONSTRUCTION Cont.

IN   OK

___ ___   FLOOR CUTS FOR PIVOT HINGE DOORS
          ___ detail keys ___ notes/refs
          coord check: ___ slab/floor ___ door sched ___ hardwr sched

___ ___   SLIDING DOOR POCKETS
          ___ dimensions ___ detail keys ___ notes/refs
          coord check: ___ wall frame ___ elec ___ hvac ___ door sched

___ ___   DOOR HARDWARE AND ATTACHMENTS 08700
          (These items are normally covered in Schedules and Specifica-
          tions, but some may be noted on floor plans of smaller build-
          ings.)

          ___ panic bars

          ___ locksets

          ___ ventilation undercuts

          ___ louvers

          ___ kickplates

          ___ "push-pull" plates

          ___ view panels

          ___ closers

          ___ mirrors

          ___ door-mounted signs

          ___ operators

          ___ name and number plates

          ___ floor-mounted doorstops

          ___ door roller bumpers where adjacent doors may hit each other

          ___ weatherstripping

          ___ light tight seals

          ___ sizes ___ detail keys ___ notes/refs
          coord check: ___ code ___ int elev ___ door sched
              ___ fin sched ___ hardwr sched ___ vent

FLOOR PLANS--FLOOR CONSTRUCTION

IN   OK

___ ___   ROUGH/NONSKID FLOOR SURFACES AT ENTRY LANDINGS, EXTERIOR STEPS
            AND ALL OTHER AREAS EXPOSED TO MOISTURE

___ ___   FINISH FLOOR MATERIAL INDICATION AND/OR NAME (Sometimes
            noted by type under each room name or number and described in
            detail in Finish Schedule and/or Specifications.)

___ ___   DIVIDING LINES AND FLOOR HEIGHT NOTES AT CHANGES IN FLOOR
            LEVEL (Note whether floor elevations apply to slab, sub-
            floor, or finish floor.)

___ ___   FLOORING PATTERNS, OR PARTIAL PLAN OF FLOORING PATTERNS

___ ___   DIRECTION OF FLOORING SEAMS OR BREAKS

___ ___   JOINT PATTERNS OF MASONRY, TILE, MARBLE, OR TERRAZZO FLOORS

___ ___   DATUM REFERENCES AT INTERIOR BALCONIES, LANDINGS, AND MEZZANINES

___ ___   RAILINGS AT FLOOR OPENINGS OR MAJOR CHANGES IN LEVEL
            ___ METAL RAILINGS (05520)
            ___ ORNAMENTAL METAL RAILINGS (05720)
            ___ WOOD RAILINGS (06440)
            ___ materials ___ dimensions ___ detail keys ___ notes/refs
            coord check: ___ code ___ floor anch ___ wall anch
                ___ struct/slab ___ int elev ___ cross sect

___ ___   STEPS
            ___ direction arrow
            ___ number of risers
            ___ handrail
            ___ materials ___ dimensions ___ detail keys ___ notes/refs
            coord check: ___ code ___ slab/floor ___ ext elev
                ___ int elev ___ cross sect

___ ___   RECESSED SUB FLOOR OR SLAB FOR TILE, MASONRY, OR TERRAZZO
            (Slab heights set for alignment of different finish floor
            materials.)
            ___ materials ___ dimensions ___ detail keys ___ notes/refs
            coord check: ___ struct frame/slab ___ cross sect
                ___ fin sched

FLOOR PLANS--FLOOR CONSTRUCTION Continued

IN   OK

___ ___ FLOOR TYPES

    ___ CONCRETE SLAB 03300 (03308)

    ___ METAL FLOOR DECK 05300 (05320)

    ___ TERRAZZO 09400 (09400)
    ___ TERRAZZO, CONDUCTIVE 09400 (09430)
    ___ TERRAZZO, PRECAST 09400 (09420)
    ___ TERRAZZO TILE 09400 (09421)

    ___ TILE 09300 (09300)
    ___ TILE, CERAMIC 09300 (09310)
    ___ TILE, CONDUCTIVE 09300 (09380)
    ___ TILE, MARBLE 09300 (09340)
    ___ TILE, QUARRY 09300 (09330)
    ___ TILE, SLATE 09300 (09332)

    ___ WOOD 09550 (09550)
    ___ WOOD STRIP 09550 (09560)
    ___ WOOD, GYMNASIUM 09550 (09561/09562)
    ___ WOOD PARQUET 09550 (09570)
    ___ WOOD, PLYWOOD BLOCK 09550 (09580)
    ___ WOOD, RESILIENT 09500 (09590)
    ___ WOOD BLOCK 09550 (09595)

    ___ STONE, FLAGSTONE 09600 (09611)
    ___ STONE, SLATE 09600 (09612)
    ___ STONE, MARBLE 09600 (09613)
    ___ STONE, GRANITE 09600 (09614)

    ___ BRICK 09600 (09620)

    ___ RESILIENT 09650 (09650)

    ___ CARPET 09680/12670 (09680/12670)

    ___ floor elevs ___ detail keys ___ notes/refs
coord check: ___ struct frame/slab ___ fin sched

FLOOR PLANS--FLOOR CONSTRUCTION Continued

IN   OK

___ ___   EXPANSION JOINTS, TOOLED JOINTS, CONSTRUCTION JOINTS, AND
            PERIMETER JOINTS IN CONCRETE SLABS 03250 (03251)
            ___ materials ___ dimensions ___ detail keys ___ notes/refs
            coord check: ___ struct frame/slab

___ ___   EXPANSION SPACE AT PERIMETER OF WOOD STRIP OR WOOD BLOCK FINISH
            FLOORING 09550 (09550)
            ___ materials ___ dimensions ___ detail keys ___ notes/refs
            coord check: ___ fin sched/base

___ ___   WOOD FLOOR PATTERN OR PATTERN DIRECTION 09550 (09550)
            (Note species if more than one is involved in pattern.)
            coord check: ___ specs ___ fin sched

___ ___   SADDLES, THRESHOLDS, METAL STRIPS SEPARATING ONE FLOOR
            MATERIAL FROM ANOTHER 05500/08700/12670 (05500/08740/12670)
            ___ materials ___ locations ___ detail keys ___ notes/refs
            coord check: ___ specs ___ fin sched

___ ___   UNDERLAYMENT FOR RESILIENT FLOORS 09650 (09650)
            ___ materials ___ notes/refs
            coord check: ___ specs ___ fin sched

___ ___   WATER AND MILDEW RESISTIVE UNDERLAYMENT BENEATH CARPET EXPOSED
            TO WATER 097680 (09680)
            ___ materials ___ dimensions ___ detail keys ___ notes/refs
            coord check: ___ specs ___ fin sched ___ plumb

___ ___   FLOOR ANCHORS FOR BUILT-INS AND EQUIPMENT 05500 (05503)
            ___ anchors for N.I.C. equipment
            ___ future equipment
            ___ materials ___ locations ___ detail keys ___ notes/refs
            coord check: ___ struct slab/floor ___ furn/equip ___ plumb
            ___ vent ___ elec

___ ___   VIBRATION PADS 13080 (13080)
            ___ curbs
            ___ pedestals
            ___ materials ___ dimensions ___ detail keys ___ notes/refs
            coord check: ___ struct slab/floor ___ hvac

___ ___   ISOLATION SLABS 13080 (13080)
            ___ materials ___ dimensions ___ detail keys ___ notes/refs
            coord check: ___ struct slab/floor ___ hvac

___ ___   FLOOR OPENINGS FOR ACCESS PANELS
            ___ materials ___ dimensions ___ detail keys ___ notes/refs
            coord check: ___ struct frame/slab ___ plumb ___ hvac

FLOOR PLANS--FLOOR CONSTRUCTION Continued

IN   OK

___ ___   BALCONIES, EXTERIOR LANDINGS, AND DECKS
          ___ floor elevation points
          ___ slopes
          ___ floor drains
          ___ hose bibbs and drains for planters
          ___ exterior surface elevation 3" below door thresholds
          ___ materials ___ dimensions ___ detail keys ___ notes/refs
          coord check: ___ struct frame/slab ___ ext elev ___ ref clg
          ___ fin sched ___ plumb/drain ___ elec

___ ___   WATERPROOF MEMBRANE CONSTRUCTION AT SHOWERS AND OTHER WET
          ROOMS 07100 (07110)
          ___ materials ___ dimensions ___ detail keys ___ notes/refs
          coord check: ___ specs ___ fin sched ___ plumb

___ ___   RAISED COMPUTER ROOM FLOOR/ACCESS FLOORING 10270 (10270)
          ___ floor grid (24" x 24" is standard)
          ___ substrate elevations finish floor elevations
          ___ stairs, ramps, and railings
          ___ plenum seal, plenum dividers
          ___ materials ___ dimensions ___ detail keys ___ notes/refs
          coord check: ___ wall anch ___ floor anch ___ int elev
          ___ cross sect ___ fin sched ___ hvac ___ elec

___ ___   CABLE, PIPE, AND DRAIN TRENCH COVER PLATES 05530 (05531)
          ___ materials ___ dimensions ___ detail keys ___ notes/refs
          coord check: ___ struct/slab ___ plumb ___ hvac ___ elec

___ ___   THRU-FLOOR SHAFTS
          ___ chases
          ___ chutes
          ___ future shafts or chases
          ___ shaft numbers
          ___ materials ___ dimensions ___ detail keys ___ notes/refs
          coord check: ___ struct frame/slab ___ ref clg ___ cross sect
          ___ plumb ___ hvac ___ elec

___ ___   CAPPED SLEEVES FOR MOVABLE STANCHIONS, OTHER PORTABLE FLOOR-
          MOUNTED FIXTURES OR EQUIPMENT 05500 (05520)
          ___ materials ___ dimensions ___ detail keys ___ notes/refs
          coord check: ___ slab/floor ___ furn ___ elec

___ ___   FLOOR DRAINS AT MECHANICAL ROOMS, GARAGES, TRASH ROOMS, TOILET
          ROOMS, COMMERCIAL KITCHENS 015400 (15421)
          ___ slope to drain
          ___ locations ___ detail keys ___ notes/refs
          coord check: ___ struct slab/floor ___ plumb ___ hvac

FLOOR PLANS--FLOOR CONSTRUCTION Continued

IN   OK

___ ___   RECESSED FRAMES FOR DOOR MATS 12670 (12673)
           ___ depth of frame and mat sinkage
           ___ materials ___ dimensions   ___ detail keys   ___ notes/refs
           coord check: ___ slab/floor

___ ___   RECESSED DOOR MAT 12670 (12675)
           ___ depth of mat sinkage
           ___ materials ___ dimensions   ___ detail keys   ___ notes/refs
           coord check: ___ slab/floor ___ fin sched

___ ___   FOOT GRILLES 12670 (12672)
           ___ depth of grille sinkage
           ___ materials ___ dimensions   ___ detail keys   ___ notes/refs
           coord check: ___ slab/floor ___ fin sched

___ ___   CONDUCTIVE FLOORS
           ___ CONDUCTIVE TERRAZZO 09400 (09430)
           ___ CONDUCTIVE RESILIENT 09650 (09675)
           ___ CONDUCTIVE ELASTOMERIC 09700 (09731)
           ___ materials ___ dimensions   ___ detail keys   ___ notes/refs
           coord check: ___ specs ___ struct slab/floor   ___ fin sched
           ___ elec

___ ___   ARMORED FLOORS 09700 (09741)
           ___ materials ___ dimensions   ___ detail keys   ___ notes/refs
           coord check: ___ specs ___ struct slab/floor   ___ fin sched

___ ___   GRATINGS 05500 (05530)
           ___ materials ___ dimensions   ___ detail keys   ___ notes/refs
           coord check: ___ struct slab/floor ___ hvac ___ elec

___ ___   FLOOR PITS
           ___ materials ___ dimensions   ___ detail keys   ___ notes/refs
           coord check: ___ struct slab/floor ___ cross sect ___ plumb
           ___ hvac ___ elec

___ ___   FLOOR PLATE PIT COVERS 05500 (05531)
           ___ materials ___ dimensions   ___ detail keys   ___ notes/refs
           coord check: ___ struct slab/floor

___ ___   CATWALKS 05500 (05530)
           ___ materials ___ dimensions   ___ detail keys   ___ notes/refs
           coord check: ___ floor anch ___ wall anch ___ ref clg
           ___ int elev ___ cross sect ___ hvac ___ elec

___ ___   SHIPS LADDERS 05500 (05516)
           ___ materials ___ dimensions   ___ detail keys   ___ notes/refs
           coord check: ___ floor anch ___ wall anch ___ int elev

FLOOR PLANS--FLOOR CONSTRUCTION Continued

IN   OK

___ ___ PIT AND MANHOLE WALL LADDERS 05500 (05515)
         ___ materials ___ dimensions ___ detail keys ___ notes/refs
         coord check: ___ floor anch ___ wall anch ___ struct
              ___ int elev ___ cross sect

___ ___ METAL SPIRAL STAIRS 05700 (05715)
         ___ materials ___ dimensions ___ detail keys ___ notes/refs
         coord check: ___ floor/wall anch ___ struct frame/slab
              ___ int elev ___ cross sect

___ ___ CAGE LADDERS 05500 (05515)
         ___ materials ___ dimensions ___ detail keys ___ notes/refs
         coord check: ___ floor anch ___ wall anch ___ struct
              ___ int elev ___ cross sect

FLOOR PLANS--TRANSPORTATION

IN   OK

___ ___   DUMBWAITERS 14100 (14101/14102)
          ___ dumbwaiter shaft number
          ___ manual or powered
          ___ dimensions ___ detail keys ___ notes/refs
          coord check: ___ struct frame ___ floor sup ___ ref clg
              ___ cross sect ___ elec

___ ___   PASSENGER ELEVATORS 14200 (14210)
          ___ elevator shaft numbers
          ___ dimensions ___ detail keys ___ notes/refs
          coord check: ___ struct frame ___ ref clg ___ roof
              ___ cross sect ___ plumb ___ hvac ___ elec

___ ___   FREIGHT ELEVATORS 14200 (14220)
          ___ elevator shaft number
          ___ dimensions ___ detail keys ___ notes/refs
          coord check: ___ struct frame ___ ref clg ___ roof
              ___ cross sect ___ plumb ___ hvac ___ elec

___ ___   MOVING WALKS 14700 (14720)
          ___ dimensions ___ detail keys ___ notes/refs
          coord check: ___ struct frame/slab ___ int elev ___ cross sect
              ___ elec

___ ___   ESCALATORS 14700 (14710)
          ___ escalator number
          ___ dimensions ___ detail keys ___ notes/refs
          coord check: ___ struct frame ___ floor sup ___ ref clg
              ___ cross sect ___ elec

___ ___   PEOPLE LIFTS 14400 (14410)
          ___ dimensions ___ detail keys ___ notes/refs
          coord check: ___ struct frame ___ floor sup ___ ref clg
              ___ cross sect ___ elec

___ ___   SIDEWALK LIFTS 14400 (14411)
          ___ dimensions ___ detail keys ___ notes/refs
          coord check: ___ struct frame/slab ___ site/paving
              ___ floor sup ___ cross sect ___ elec

___ ___   WHEELCHAIR LIFTS 14400 (14415)
          ___ dimensions ___ detail keys ___ notes/refs
          coord check: ___ struct frame ___ floor sup ___ cross sect
              ___ elec

FLOOR PLANS--TRANSPORTATION Continued

IN   OK

___ ___ VEHICLE LIFTS 14400 (14450)
         ___ dimensions ___ detail keys ___ notes/refs
         coord check: ___ struct frame ___ floor sup ___ cross sect
             ___ elec

___ ___ PNEUMATIC TUBES 14500 (14581)
         ___ dimensions ___ detail keys ___ notes/refs
         coord check: ___ struct frame ___ ref clg ___ cross sect
             ___ elec

FLOOR PLANS--STAIRWAYS

Verify requirements and exit regulations with local code. Check stair
widths for furniture access. The minimum headroom clearance between
nosing and soffit is 6'-6".

IN   OK

___ ___   TREADS AND RISERS
            ___ risers 7-1/2" maximum, treads 10" minimum
            ___ maximum deviation in riser heights and tread width in a
                single flight is 3/16"
            ___ materials ___ dimensions ___ detail keys ___ notes/refs
            coord check: ___ code ___ stair sect

___ ___   NONSLIP TREADS
            ___ detail keys ___ notes/refs
            coord check: ___ code

___ ___   HANDRAILS AT EACH SIDE OF STAIR
            (Terminate railings onto newels or return to wall to avoid
             sleeve catchers. Handrail, beam, or other projections should
             not reduce required clear width by more than 3-1/2".)
            ___ METAL 05500 (05520)
            ___ WOOD 06400 (06440)
            ___ materials ___ dimensions ___ detail keys ___ notes/refs
            coord check: ___ code ___ wall anch ___ stair sect

___ ___   RAILING POST POCKETS IN CONCRETE STAIRS 05500 (05520)
            (Located and designed to avoid spalling of concrete.)
            ___ materials ___ dimensions ___ detail keys ___ notes/refs
            coord check: ___ code ___ floor anch ___ wall anch
                         ___ stair sect

___ ___   RAILINGS 05500 (05520)
            ___ floor openings
            ___ open landings
            ___ glazed walls near landings
            ___ materials ___ dimensions ___ detail keys ___ notes/refs
            coord check: ___ code ___ floor anch ___ wall anch
                         ___ stair sect

___ ___   LANDINGS: MINIMUM 1 EACH 12' OF VERTICAL STAIR RUN
            (Minimum landing width in direction of travel is equal to
             stair width.)
            ___ stair landing elevation points
            ___ materials ___ dimensions ___ detail keys ___ notes/refs
            coord check: ___ code ___ wall anch ___ stair pl/sect

FLOOR PLANS--STAIRWAYS Continued

IN   OK

___ ___   STAIRWELL LANDING WALL CORNERS ROUNDED, ANGLED, OR WITH
          GUIDE RAILS TO AID FLOW OF EXIT TRAFFIC
          ___ materials ___ dimensions ___ detail keys ___ notes/refs
          coord check: ___ code ___ wall anch ___ stair pl/sect

___ ___   BATTERY-POWERED EMERGENCY ILLUMINATION 16600 (16613)
          ___ locations ___ detail keys ___ notes/refs
          coord check: ___ code ___ wall anch ___ ref clg ___ elec

___ ___   UNDER-STAIR SOFFIT MATERIAL AND CONSTRUCTION
          ___ materials ___ dimensions ___ detail keys ___ notes/refs
          coord check: ___ stair pl/sect ___ int elev ___ fin sched

___ ___   UNDER-STAIR STORAGE ROOM
          ___ materials ___ dimensions ___ detail keys ___ notes/refs
          coord check: ___ stair pl/sect ___ fin sched ___ elec

___ ___   UNDER-STAIR ACCESS DOOR
          ___ materials ___ dimensions ___ detail keys ___ notes/refs
          coord check: ___ int elev ___ door sched

___ ___   GUTTERS, DRAINS, AND GRATINGS WHERE STAIRS ARE EXPOSED TO
          WEATHER 02400 (02400)
          ___ materials ___ dimensions ___ detail keys ___ notes/refs
          coord check: ___ stair pl/sect ___ site/drain

FLOOR PLANS--DIMENSIONING

IN   OK

___ ___   GENERAL NOTES ABOUT THE DIMENSIONING SYSTEM
          ___ modular dimensioning practice and conventions
          ___ whether dimensions are to finish surfaces, to rough
              surfaces, or to framing
          ___ special arrowhead indications if using coded dimensioning

___ ___   LEGEND OF DIMENSION NOTES
          ___ n.t.s. ___ "varies" ___ +/- ___ "eq" ___ "typ"

___ ___   FINISH GRADE ELEVATION POINTS AT CORNERS AND PERIMETER OF
           BUILDING

___ ___   OVERALL EXTERIOR WALL LENGTHS

___ ___   OFFSETS

___ ___   PROJECTIONS

___ ___   RECESSES

___ ___   SIZES OF REMOVABLE EXTERIOR WALL PANELS

___ ___   EXTERIOR OPENINGS (Openings that clearly center on bays or
           are adjacent to columns often don't require dimensioning;
           door and window sizes may be covered in Schedules.)

___ ___   INTERIOR WALL AND PARTITION LENGTHS

___ ___   DISTANCES BETWEEN INTERIOR WALLS OR PARTITIONS IN DIMENSION
           STRINGS ACROSS LENGTH AND WIDTH OF BUILDING (Dimension strings
           are located so as not to conflict with other essential notes,
           such as room names or numbers. Parallel strings of dimensions
           on interior plans are not considered desirable.)

___ ___   COLUMN, POST, AND MULLION CENTER-LINE DIMENSIONS

___ ___   CUMULATIVE DIMENSION NOTES AT COLUMN LINES

___ ___   DIMENSIONS OF OVERHANGS AND OVERHEAD PROJECTIONS

___ ___   THICKNESSES OF EXTERIOR WALLS AND INTERIOR PARTITIONS
           (Interior partitions are often dimensioned to center lines.)

FLOOR PLANS--DIMENSIONING Continued

IN   OK

___ ___   DIMENSIONS OR DIMENSION NOTES

____ chases

____ furred walls

____ shafts

____ future shafts

____ small thru-wall openings, length and height

____ built-ins, sizes and dimensions to finished surfaces

___ ___   HEIGHT OR ELEVATION NOTES

____ grades

____ rough flooring

____ rails

____ height of sills of openings above floor

____ countertops

____ built-ins

____ fixtures

____ low partitions

___ ___ SPACINGS OF PLUMBING FIXTURES

___ ___ RADII OF ARCS WITH REFERENCE DIMENSIONS TO LOCATE CENTERS OF
ARCS OR CIRCLES

___ ___ ANGLES IN DEGREES OF NON-RIGHT ANGLE WALLS AND BUILT-INS
(In lieu of degree measurements, ends of angled unit or wall
may be dimensioned from reference line or wall.)

___ ___ CENTER LINES OF SYMMETRICAL PLANS WITH NOTE THAT DIMENSIONS
ARE TYPICAL FOR AREAS ON BOTH SIDES OF THE CENTER LINE

CHAPTER FOUR--ROOF PLANS   4.0 - 4.11

        CHAPTER CONTENTS:

        Items That Should be Avoided on Roof
          Plan Drawings   4.1
        Coordination   4.1 - 4.2
        Items Suited to Systems Drafting, Paste-
          up, and Overlay   4.2

        General Reference Information   4.3

        Construction Components   4.4 - 4.11

ROOF PLANS--INTRODUCTION

The roof plan is usually the simplest type of plan drawing, but its subject is the source of 30% to 50% of all lawsuits against design firms.
The quality of a roofing installation is primarily established by specifications, flashing and roofing details, and stringent construction
administration.

Roof plans are mainly for showing slopes, drainage, junctures of change
in roof materials or construction, roof appurtenances such as bulkheads,
and most importantly, to identify and reference all relevant construction detailing.

Besides inadequate detailing and improper roofing application, the most
common roofing problem is inadequate drainage. Roofing slopes are often
minimal, and they flatten out more during construction. Later the flat
areas become undrainable ponds after the building settles. Even if
the drain slopes are generous, often enough the drains themselves are
inadequate in number and size.

ITEMS THAT SHOULD BE AVOIDED ON ROOF PLAN DRAWINGS

____ Roofing notes tend to be overly specific, and often duplicate or
     contradict the specifications. Use simple generic identification
     notes, and leave exact materials, gauges, and application instruc-
     tions for specifications.

____ Roof framing should usually be drawn on its own sheet and not com-
     bined with the roof plan. The purpose of the roof plan is to show
     finish construction, and it can be confusing when finish work is
     mixed in with structure or substructure. However, it is useful to
     combine framing and finished roofing as base and overlay sheets.
     Then framing can be printed as a screened background shadow print
     to show its coordination with major features of the roof.

____ Drafters sometimes get overly decorative on special roof textures
     and materials indications. Use only partial indications of tex-
     turing.

COORDINATION

____ Roof plans should be directly derived from the uppermost building
     floor plan by means of overlay drafting or by use of reproducible
     background sheets. If using overlay drafting, you can print final
     roof plans with a screened shadow print of the upper floor plan
     as background reference for solid-line roof construction. That
     will help assure 100% one-to-one coordination between floor plan
     and roof.

ROOF PLANS--INTRODUCTION Continued

COORDINATION Continued

____ The main coordination trouble spots usually occur in the relationship of the roof plan with structural drawings, with plumbing
drawings showing interior roof drains and rain water leaders, and
with building drainage at the sitework level.

____ The most crucial coordination trouble spot is the relationship of
roof plan and roof details to specifications. Details are frequently drawn (copied) by unqualified junior or intermediate level
drafting staff members and often fail to fit the building situation
they're supposedly designed for. Specifications, even if correct,
often fail to agree with the drawings, which creates another facet
of the problem. In checking the roof plan and roofing details,
specifications should be read virtually side by side with the
drawings.

ITEMS SUITED TO SYSTEMS DRAFTING, PASTE-UP, AND OVERLAY

____ As noted above, roof plans should be created as overlay sheets in
direct one-to-one reference to upper floor plans. This not only
maximizes coordination between roof, floor, and consultants' plans,
it allows the use of shadow prints to show the upper floor plan as
a screened background image in contrast to solid-line roof plan
data.

____ Roof construction details are highly standardizable and should be
a large part of the office's master and reference detail library.
As you complete roofing details on a variety of projects, consider
creating an overall standard detail sheet with a variety of details
reusable from job to job.

____ If the roofing work includes repair or remodeling, use photo drafting. Combine photographs of existing conditions with line drawing
and notation of new work.

____ Since the notation on roof plans tends to be sparse but highly repetitive, it's especially convenient to use note numbers linked to
a keynote legend on the side of the drawing. Consider attaching
detail keys to the same legend, to combine both types of data.

____ Small unit appliques and tape drafting are especially suited to
the small symbols and special line work that's common to roof
plans. "Slope" with arrow indication, and section/detail reference bubbles are typical of preprinted elements that can be
applied to these drawings as appliques or paste-ups.

ROOF PLANS--GENERAL REFERENCE INFORMATION

IN   OK

___ ___   BUILDING OUTLINE AND ROOF OUTLINE
(Broken-line building perimeter where shown below roof overhang.)

___ ___   OVERALL EXTERIOR WALL DIMENSIONS

___ ___   ROOF OVERHANG DIMENSIONS

___ ___   OUTLINE OF FUTURE ADDITIONS

___ ___   CONNECTION WITH EXISTING STRUCTURES

___ ___   BUILDING AND ROOF EAVE DIMENSIONS

___ ___   DIMENSIONS TO PROPERTY LINES

___ ___   BUILDING LOCATION REFERENCED TO BENCH MARK

___ ___   REQUIRED PROPERTY SETBACK LINES

___ ___   ALL PROJECTIONS LABELED AND DIMENSIONED SHOWING COMPLIANCE
WITH PROPERTY LINE AND SETBACK REQUIREMENTS

___ ___   STAIR NUMBERS

___ ___   OUTLINE OF OPENINGS AND PROJECTIONS
___   bays
___   areaways
___   balconies
___   marquees
___   canopies
___   landings
___   decks
___   steps
___   sills
___   materials ___ dimensions ___ detail keys ___ notes/refs

ROOF PLANS--CONSTRUCTION COMPONENTS

All items are assumed to require cross-checking with architectural floor
plans, so those "coord checks" aren't listed. Most items are also assumed to require coordination checking with specifications, so that note
is included only on the most critical items.

Coordination checks with structural drawings are listed along with many
other cross-checks that are most commonly overlooked.

IN   OK

___ ___   LOWER STORY CANOPIES AND MARQUEES (10530)
          ___ slopes
          ___ drains and scuppers
          ___ materials ___ dimensions ___ detail keys ___ notes/refs
          coord check: ___ code ___ struct ___ wall anch ___ ext elev
               ___ cross sect

___ ___   UPPER FLOOR BALCONIES
          ___ drain slopes
          ___ drains and scuppers
          ___ materials ___ dimensions ___ detail keys ___ notes/refs
          coord check: ___ struct ___ wall anch ___ ext elev
               ___ cross sect

___ ___   ROOF DRAINS 15400 (15422)
          ___ locations ___ detail keys ___ notes/refs
          coord check: ___ plumb ___ struct ___ roof anch ___ site

___ ___   SCUPPERS 07600 (07633)
          ___ locations ___ detail keys ___ notes/refs
          coord check: ___ site drain ___ roof anch

___ ___   ROOF GUTTERS 07600 (07631)
          ___ gutter screens
          ___ expansion joints
          ___ slopes and directions of slopes
          ___ materials ___ dimensions ___ detail keys ___ notes/refs
          coord check: ___ site drain ___ roof anch

___ ___   DOWNSPOUTS AND RAIN WATER LEADERS 07600 (07632)
          ___ strainers at tops of leaders
          ___ rain diverters
          ___ overflows
          ___ materials ___ dimensions ___ detail keys ___ notes/refs
          coord check: ___ site drain ___ roof anch

___ ___   ROOF SLOPES: DIRECTION OF SLOPES AND DEGREE IN INCHES PER FOOT
          ___ valleys
          ___ hips
          ___ ridges
          coord check: ___ struct ___ ext elev ___ cross sect
               ___ site drain

ROOF PLANS--CONSTRUCTION COMPONENTS Continued

IN   OK

___ ___   GRAVEL STOPS 07600 (07660)
            ___ expansion joints
            ___ materials ___ detail keys ___ notes/refs
            coord check: ___ specs ___ wall sect

___ ___   FASCIAS
            ___ CONCRETE 03400 (03450)
            ___ TERRA COTTA 04200 (04251)
            ___ METAL 05700 (05730)
            ___ WOOD 06200 (06260)
            ___ materials ___ dimensions ___ detail keys ___ notes/refs
            coord check: ___ ext elev ___ wall sect

___ ___   EXPANSION JOINTS AND EXPANSION JOINT COVERS 05800
            (05802 to 05805)
            ___ materials ___ detail keys ___ notes/refs
            coord check: ___ specs ___ struct ___ cross sect

___ ___   EAVE SNOW GUARDS 07600 (07635)
            ___ materials ___ dimensions ___ detail keys ___ notes/refs
            coord check: ___ struct ___ roof anch ___ drain ___ cross sect

___ ___   PARAPETS
            ___ CONCRETE 03300/03400 (03300/03400)
            ___ MASONRY 04200 (04200)
            ___ METAL FRAME 05100 (05160/05400)
            ___ WOOD FRAME 06100 (06100)
            ___ expansion joints
            ___ materials ___ dimensions ___ detail keys ___ notes/refs
            coord check: ___ struct ___ ext elev ___ cross sect
                 ___ wall sect

___ ___   PARAPET FLASHING 07600 (07603/07604)
            ___ materials ___ detail keys ___ notes/refs
            coord check: ___ specs ___ wall sect

___ ___   PARAPET CAP FLASHING 07600 (07603)
            ___ materials ___ detail keys ___ notes/refs
            coord check: ___ specs ___ ext elev ___ cross sect
                 ___ wall sect

ROOF PLANS--CONSTRUCTION COMPONENTS Continued

IN OK

___ ___ ROOF FRAMING
         (Sometimes shown in partial plan view.)
         ___ CONCRETE 03300/03400 (03300/03400)
         ___ STEEL 05100 (05100)
         ___ WOOD 06100 (06100)
         ___ girders
         ___ beams
         ___ joists
         ___ rafters
         ___ trusses
         ___ purlins
         ___ joist bridging
         ___ materials ___ sizes/spacings ___ detail keys
              ___ notes/refs
         coord check: ___ struct ___ hvac ___ plumb ___ cross sect
              ___ wall sect

___ ___ ROOF SHEATHING 06100 (06113)
         (Often shown in partial plan view.)
         ___ detail keys ___ notes/refs
         coord check: ___ specs ___ cross sect ___ wall sect

___ ___ FINISH ROOFING MATERIALS
         ___ ASPHALT SHINGLES 07300 (07311)
         ___ BUILT-UP ROOF 07500 (07510)
         ___ CLAY TILES 07300 (07321)
         ___ CONCRETE TILES 07300 (07322)
         ___ MEMBRANE ROOF 07500 (07500)
         ___ METAL SHINGLES 07300 (07316)
         ___ SHEET METAL 07600 (07610)
         ___ SLATE SHINGLES 07300 (07314)
         ___ WOOD SHINGLES/SHAKES 07300 (07313)
         ___ PREFORMED METAL ROOFING 07400 (07412)
         ___ detail keys ___ notes/refs
         coord check: ___ specs ___ ext elev ___ cross sect

___ ___ WOOD DECK OR DUCKBOARD 06100 (06125)
         ___ dimensions ___ detail keys ___ notes/refs
         coord check: ___ roof anch

___ ___ JOGGING TRACK/ATHLETIC SURFACES 02500 (02535/02540)
         ___ materials ___ dimensions ___ detail keys ___ notes/refs
         coord check: ___ specs ___ struct

___ ___ ROOF INSULATON 07200 (07220)
         ___ materials ___ detail keys ___ notes/refs
         coord check: ___ specs ___ hvac ___ cross sect

ROOF PLANS--CONSTRUCTION COMPONENTS   Continued

IN   OK

___ ___   SKYLIGHTS 07800 (07810 to 07812)
          ___ curb and cant strip lines at skylights
          ___ wire mesh guards
          ___ materials ___ dimensions ___ detail keys ___ notes/refs
          coord check: ___ struct ___ hvac ___ ext elev ___ cross sect

___ ___   MONITORS/ROOF WINDOWS 08650 (08655)
          ___ materials ___ dimensions ___ detail keys ___ notes/refs
          coord check: ___ struct ___ hvac ___ ext elev ___ cross sect

___ ___   ROOF OPENINGS
          ___ light wells
          ___ atriums
          ___ courts
          ___ shafts
          ___ shaft numbers
          ___ shaft roofs
          ___ railings at open shafts
          ___ dimensions ___ detail keys ___ notes/refs
          coord check: ___ struct ___ roof anch ___ hvac ___ cross sect

___ ___   PLUMBING STACKS 15400 (15405)
          ___ locations ___ detail keys ___ notes/refs
          coord check: ___ plumb ___ hvac

___ ___   AIR HANDLING VENTS 15800 (15800)
          (Air intakes located 10' minimum from soil stack vents. Intakes
           and exhausts set at height to avoid clogging by snow.)
          ___ air intakes
          ___ exhaust vents
          ___ roof ventilators
          ___ ridge vents
          ___ dimensions ___ detail keys ___ notes/refs
          coord check: ___ hvac ___ struct ___ roof anch ___ elec

___ ___   BREATHER VENTS 07800 (07825)
          ___ materials ___ dimensions ___ detail keys ___ notes/refs
          coord check: ___ specs ___ wall sect

___ ___   SMOKE VENT HATCHES 07800 (07831)
          ___ materials ___ dimensions ___ detail keys ___ notes/refs
          coord check: ___ code ___ struct ___ hvac ___ elec

___ ___   ROOF-MOUNTED HVAC EQUIPMENT 15650/15800 (15650/15800)
          ___ dimensions ___ detail keys ___ notes/refs
          coord check: ___ hvac ___ plumb ___ struct ___ roof anch

ROOF PLANS--CONSTRUCTION COMPONENTS Continued

IN   OK

___ ___   EXPOSED DUCTWORK 15800 (15840)
            ___ dimensions ___ detail keys ___ notes/refs
            coord check: ___ hvac ___ struct ___ roof anch

___ ___   CHIMNEYS
            ___ MASONRY 04200 (04210)
            ___ PREFAB 10300 (10301)
            ___ flues
            ___ spark arresters
            ___ coping caps
            ___ chimney coping block or cement wash, slope toward flue
            ___ materials ___ dimensions ___ detail keys ___ notes/refs
            coord check: ___ code ___ struct ___ ext elev ___ hvac
                ___ cross sect ___ wall sect

___ ___   CHIMNEY FLASHING 07600 (07608)
            ___ saddle
            ___ cricket
            ___ materials ___ detail keys ___ notes/refs
            coord check: ___ specs

___ ___   ELEVATOR PENTHOUSE/MACHINE ROOM 14200 (14200)
            ___ elevator shaft vent
            ___ roof slope and drainage
            ___ materials ___ dimensions ___ detail keys ___ notes/refs
            coord check: ___ elev sect ___ struct ___ ext elev
                ___ cross sect ___ elec

___ ___   SMOKE VENT PENTHOUSES 07800 (07831)
            ___ smoke vent hatches
            ___ drains
            ___ materials ___ dimensions ___ detail keys ___ notes/refs
            coord check: ___ hvac ___ struct ___ ext elev ___ cross sect

___ ___   ROOF HATCHES 07800 (07830)
            ___ materials ___ dimensions ___ detail keys ___ notes/refs
            coord check: ___ struct ___ hvac ___ cross sect
                ___ wall sect

___ ___   FIRE ESCAPES 05500 (05514)
            ___ materials ___ dimensions ___ detail keys ___ notes/refs
            coord check: ___ code ___ struct ___ ext elev ___ roof anch
                ___ wall sect

___ ___   STAIR BULKHEADS
            ___ materials ___ dimensions ___ detail keys ___ notes/refs
            coord check: ___ stair sect ___ ext elev ___ cross sect

ROOF PLANS--CONSTRUCTION COMPONENTS Continued

IN   OK

___ ___ OUTWARD OPENING DOORS ONTO ROOF
          ___ curb
          ___ overhead weather protection
          ___ light
          coord check: ___ stair sect ___ door sched ___ elec

___ ___ RAILINGS 05500 (05520)
          ___ materials ___ detail keys ___ notes/refs
          coord check: ___ code ___ struct ___ roof anch ___ wall sect
               ___ ext elev

___ ___ ROOF LADDERS 05500 (05517)
          ___ materials ___ dimensions ___ detail keys ___ notes/refs
          coord check: ___ struct ___ roof anch ___ ext elev
               ___ cross sect ___ wall sect

___ ___ WINDOW WASHING EQUIPMENT PENTHOUSE 11010 (11012)
          ___ materials ___ dimensions ___ detail keys ___ notes/refs
          coord check: ___ struct ___ ext elev ___ cross sect
               ___ plumb ___ elec

___ ___ PIPE RAIL AND GATE FOR WINDOW WASHING EQUIPMENT 11010 (11012)
          ___ materials ___ dimensions ___ detail keys ___ notes/refs
          coord check: ___ struct ___ roof anch ___ ext elev ___ plumb
               ___ cross sect ___ elec

___ ___ FLAGPOLES 10350 (10360)
          ___ flood lights
          ___ locations ___ detail keys ___ notes/refs
          coord check: ___ struct ___ roof anch ___ ext elev ___ elec

___ ___ LIGHTNING RODS 16600 (16601)
          ___ locations ___ detail keys ___ notes/refs
          coord check: ___ ext elev ___ elec

___ ___ COOLING TOWERS 15650 (15650)
          ___ materials ___ dimensions ___ detail keys ___ notes/refs
          coord check: ___ struct ___ hvac ___ plumb ___ elec
               ___ ext elev ___ cross sect

___ ___ COOLING TOWER PENTHOUSE
          ___ cooling tower exhaust located 100' away from all air intakes
          ___ materials ___ dimensions ___ detail keys ___ notes/refs
          coord check: ___ struct ___ hvac ___ plumb ___ ext elev
               ___ cross sect

ROOF PLANS--CONSTRUCTION COMPONENTS Continued

IN   OK

___ ___   SOUND AND VIBRATION ISOLATION BETWEEN ROOF-TOP EQUIPMENT
           AND ROOMS AT STORY BELOW ROOF 15200 (15200)
           ___ materials ___ dimensions ___ detail keys ___ notes/refs
           coord check: ___ hvac ___ struct ___ acoust

___ ___   IDENTIFICATION OR DIRECTION MARKER FOR AIRCRAFT
           ___ dimensions ___ notes/refs
           coord check: ___ code

___ ___   DECORATIVE PAVING/GRAVEL PATTERNS
           ___ dimensions ___ notes/refs
           coord check: ___ specs

___ ___   SOLAR HEAT COLLECTION PANELS 13980 (13980)
           ___ materials ___ dimensions ___ detail keys ___ notes/refs
           coord check: ___ struct ___ roof anch ___ hvac ___ plumb
           ___ elec ___ ext elev ___ cross sect

___ ___   SOLAR WATER HEATERS 13980/15400 (13980/15431)
           ___ materials ___ dimensions ___ detail keys ___ notes/refs
           coord check: ___ struct ___ roof anch ___ hvac ___ plumb
           ___ elec ___ ext elev ___ cross sect

___ ___   WATER TANKS 13400/15400 (13410/15400)
           ___ materials ___ dimensions ___ detail keys ___ notes/refs
           coord check: ___ plumb ___ struct ___ roof anch

___ ___   ROOF PLUMBING 15400/15500 (15400/15500)
           ___ hose bibbs
           ___ hydrants
           ___ standpipes
           ___ piping supports
           ___ stub ups
           ___ locations ___ detail keys ___ notes/refs
           coord check: ___ plumb ___ struct ___ roof anch ___ hvac

___ ___   CABLE SERVICE ENTRIES 16400/16700
           (Overhead power, TV cable, and phone lines located to clear
            driveways or walkways at legally required heights.)
           ___ ELECTRICAL SERVICE ENTRY 16400 (16401)
           ___ TELEPHONE CABLE ENTRY 16700 (16740)
           ___ TV CABLE ENTRY 16700 (16780)
           ___ locations ___ detail keys ___ notes/refs
           coord check: ___ code ___ util ___ site

ROOF PLANS--CONSTRUCTION COMPONENTS   Continued

IN   OK

___ ___   SUPPORTS AND GUYS FOR OVERHEAD CABLE   07800   (07871)
              ___ locations ___ detail keys ___ notes/refs
          coord check: ___ elec ___ roof anch

___ ___   OVERHEAD CABLE PERISCOPE ENTRY HEADS   16400   (16401/16420)
              ___ mounting pockets for entry heads
              ___ locations ___ detail keys ___ notes/refs
          coord check: ___ site ___ util ___ roof anch

___ ___   WEATHERPROOF ELECTRIC OUTLETS   16050   (16134)
              ___ locations ___ notes/refs

___ ___   EXTERIOR BUILDING LIGHTING   16500   (16520)
              ___ locations ___ detail keys ___ notes/refs
          coord check: ___ roof anch ___ elec

___ ___   AIRCRAFT WARNING LIGHTS   16500   (16560)
              ___ locations ___ detail keys ___ notes/refs
          coord check: ___ code ___ struct ___ roof anch ___ elec

___ ___   ROOF ANTENNA
              ___ TV TOWER MASTER ANTENNA   16700   (16781)
              ___ SATELLITE DISH ANTENNA   11800   (11800)
              ___ BROADCAST ANTENNA   16700   (16790)
              ___ locations ___ detail keys ___ notes/refs
          coord check: ___ code ___ struct ___ roof anch ___ elec

___ ___   ROOF-MOUNTED SIGNS   10400   (10430 to 10440)
              ___ materials ___ dimensions ___ detail keys ___ notes/refs
          coord check: ___ code ___ struct ___ roof anch ___ elec

___ ___   GUY WIRE ANCHORS FOR ANTENNA, SIGNS, AND OTHER FIXTURES
          07800   (07871)
              ___ locations ___ detail keys ___ notes/refs
          coord check: ___ struct ___ roof anch

___ ___   WEATHER VANES   05700   (05745)
              ___ locations ___ detail keys ___ notes/refs
          coord check: ___ roof anch

___ ___   PREFABRICATED ROOF SPECIALTIES
              ___ STEEPLES   10340   (10341)
              ___ SPIRES   10340   (10342)
              ___ CUPOLAS   10340   (10343)
              ___ materials ___ dimensions ___ detail keys ___ notes/refs
          coord check: ___ struct ___ roof anch ___ ext elev

CHAPTER FIVE--EXTERIOR ELEVATIONS   5.0 - 5.20

EXTERIOR ELEVATIONS--INTRODUCTION

The primary purpose of the exterior elevations is to show heights of exterior construction elements. Despite this, important heights are often excluded, particularly heights of sills, lintels, thru-wall sleeves and openings, etc. The other most common omissions are "partial elevation" views of walls within small recesses or extensions.

Exterior elevations are most important to the designer in terms of showing design intent: forms, proportions, composition of exterior patterns and textures, etc. Their primary value to the contractor is to show heights and to identify junctures, joints, and boundaries of materials. This divergence in design intent and construction need is the source of most elevation errors and omissions. Double check that final elevations are elaborated upon specifically with construction data foremost in mind.

ITEMS THAT SHOULD BE AVOIDED ON EXTERIOR ELEVATION DRAWINGS

____ The most common area of overdrawing is the inclusion of door and window symbols referenced to schedules and details. Except possibly in the smallest of building designs, doors and windows should be referenced strictly on the plans. Any further referencing in elevations will either be unnecessary duplicated labor or a source of error and contradiction as changes accumulate on plans which are not picked up in elevations.

____ Another common kind of overdrawing is the inclusion of sill/jamb/head detail keys for doors and windows. Those detail keys should be in the door and window schedule frame drawings, not on plans or elevations. (A plan or exterior elevation detail key at doors or windows is justified only to call attention to one-of-a-kind construction conditions.)

____ Exterior elevations are frequently drawn at much larger scale than required for the information shown. For best speed and accuracy, elevations should be derived from direct, one-to-one overlay take off from the exterior walls shown on the plans. Thus both plans and elevations should be at the same scale and should be drawn at the smallest practical size. (This assumes other graphic simplifications have been implemented to make sure the plans are not crowded and cluttered.)

____ Use only partial indications of materials and textures, and single-line (or double-line at most) outlines of doors, windows, etc. A possible exception would be when using preprinted texture applique or paste-up sheets. But even then, partial cut-line views of materials, patterns and textures are preferred both for speed and graphic clarity. (Large-scale drawings tend to encourage over-elaboration since they otherwise tend to look empty and unfinished.)

EXTERIOR ELEVATIONS--INTRODUCTION Continued

COORDINATION

____ The exterior elevations should be derived directly, by overlay comparison and tracing of exterior wall elements from the plans. Drafters often attempt to measure and draw elevations without direct tracing from plans and usually make errors in the process.

____ Minor side views of recesses in the perimeter of a building are often overlooked. Double-check for small partial views.

____ If the exterior elevations show broken-line indications of below-grade construction, they should also be directly overlaid with foundation and/or basement plans in drawing and checking.

____ Do overlay comparisons of exterior elevations with structural draw-ings to verify structurally framed opening locations and sizes and the locations of vertical expansion or construction joints.

____ Do overlay comparisons of exterior elevations with roof plans to coordinate roof overhangs, visible roof slopes, and visible roof-mounted components.

____ Use overlay comparisons of exterior elevations with mechanical drawings to verify locations of air intakes, exhausts, hydrants, standpipes, exterior-mounted mechanical equipment, roof mechanical room and cooling tower sizes, etc.

____ Use overlay comparisons of exterior elevations with electrical drawings to verify exterior lighting, illuminated signage, exte-rior-mounted powered equipment, etc.

____ Use overlay comparisons of exterior elevations with roof plans to verify location of visible rainwater leaders. Compare loca-tions with building perimeter drainage shown on site plans.

____ Compare exterior elevations with site plans to identify any at-tached or nearby site improvements such as walls, fences, walk-way canopies, etc. that should be shown with exterior views of the building.

____ Compare exterior elevations with site plans to identify any site construction such as walls, kiosks, gazebos, fences, etc. that may require separate exterior elevation views.

____ Design or drafting staff don't always know whether the building's "north" elevation is supposed to face north or if the viewer is facing north. The office should have a stated rule in the draft-ing manual, and this rule should also be included as a general note on the drawings. Otherwise, and preferably, include number or letter symbols for all exterior views and show them on mini-ature key plans on all plan, elevation and section sheets.

EXTERIOR ELEVATIONS--INTRODUCTION   Continued

ITEMS SUITED TO SYSTEMS DRAFTING, PASTE-UP, AND OVERLAY

____ Exterior elevations usually include repetitive fenestration, materials patterns, etc., all highly conducive to paste-up drafting. Each common repetitive element should be identified as early as possible and printed in multiple for paste-up.

____ Exterior elevation views often include large areas of repetition from one view to another. In such cases, create the original view paste-up and then contact print that in whole or part as the starter for other elevation paste-ups. An alternative is to use one view as a base sheet and do any variations on overlays. The latter alternative is most appropriate when virtually every view of the building is identical, as say, in the case of a square plan curtain wall office building.

____ When exterior elevations or variations of exterior designs are completed for presentation drawings, do all rendering and studies of design options on overlays. Allow no notation or rendering elements on the original elevation drawings or paste-ups. After final design revisions, use the uncluttered plain-line drawings as base sheets for working drawing overlays. Do dimensions, detail and section keys, titles, materials indications and architectural notation on overlays. Often the same overlay information will be reusable for one or more additional views of the building.

____ Materials indications and textures can be applied as dry transfer rub-ons or thin stickyback films. Applique manufacturers offer a huge variety of textures and indications--from brick to foliage and dots to crosshatching--which are suited to both renderings and working drawings.

____ By keeping base sheets uncluttered with architectural notes, you can combine screened shadow print images of the elevations with solid-line cross section drawings. Also, they'll remain readily adaptable to reuse and change if major revisions come up.

____ If the drawings include additions or remodeling work, make screened shadow print images of the existing conditions as background, and show new work in solid line. Similarly, if drawings include alternate or phased construction, use the combination of screened lines and solid-line overlay combinations to clearly separate base contract work from alternates, or first phase work from later construction.

____ Notes for exterior elevations are highly repetitive from view to view, so you can readily use one keynote legend and bubble reference all notation in the field of the drawing by number. In lieu of keynoting, you can create one or more strips of notes and copy them as stickybacks or paste-ups onto each elevation view.

EXTERIOR ELEVATIONS--GENERAL REFERENCE INFORMATION

IN   OK

___ ___ DRAWING TITLE AND SCALE

___ ___ SHEET NUMBER AT TITLE BLOCK

___ ___ TITLES OR SYMBOL KEYS TO IDENTIFY EACH ELEVATION VIEW

___ ___ KEY PLAN SHOWING NORTH ARROW AND ELEVATION VIEW LOCATIONS

___ ___ MODULAR GRID OR STRUCTURAL COLUMN GRID WITH NUMBER AND LETTER
            COORDINATES

___ ___ PROPERTY LINES

___ ___ SETBACK LINES

___ ___ OUTLINE OF ADJACENT STRUCTURES

___ ___ OUTLINE OF FUTURE BUILDING ADDITIONS

___ ___ MATCH UP LINE, OVERLAP LINE, AND REFERENCE IF DRAWING IS
            CONTINUED ON ANOTHER SHEET

___ ___ ITEMS N.I.C., N.I.C ITEMS INSTALLED OR CONNECTED BY CONTRACTOR

___ ___ REMODELING
            ___ work to be removed   ___ work to remain
            ___ work to be repaired ___ work to be relocated

___ ___ GENERAL NOTES

___ ___ BUILDING CODE REFERENCES

___ ___ DRAWING CROSS REFERENCES

___ ___ SPECIFICATION REFERENCES

___ ___ CROSS SECTION LINES AND KEYS

___ ___ WALL SECTION LINES AND KEYS

___ ___ MATERIALS HATCHING OR POCHE (Use only partial materials
            indications on building area.)

___ ___ DETAIL KEYS (Not for doors, windows or storefront details.
            Those details are to be referenced from schedules, not
            elevations or plans.)

EXTERIOR ELEVATIONS--SUBGRADE TO FLOOR LINE

Suggested coordination checks are included for this portion of exterior elevations. Most of the necessary coordination checks for exterior
elevations at grade level can also be found in the site plans checklist.

Other portions of exterior elevations will have the same coordination
checks as their equivalent parts on the floor plans. When checking
those portions of elevation drawings, check floor plans first, then
move on to exterior elevations.

IN   OK

____ ____ EXISTING AND NEW FINISH GRADE LINE AND ELEVATIONS
          (Rough grade, finish grade, and topsoil depth sometimes shown.)
          ____ fill and engineered fill
          ____ crushed rock fill
          coord check: ____ civil/soil

____ ____ EXISTING UNDERGROUND STRUCTURES
          ____ to remain
          ____ to be repaired
          ____ to be removed
          ____ materials ____ dimensions ____ detail keys ____ notes/refs
          coord check: ____ civil/soil ____ struct ____ const plan
                        ____ site/drain

____ ____ HOLES, TRENCHES, EXCAVATIONS TO BE FILLED 02200 (02221)
          ____ locations/sizes ____ elevation points ____ notes/refs
          coord check: ____ civil/soil ____ landscape ____ site/drain

____ ____ EXISTING ROCK OUTCROPS TO BE REMOVED 02200 (02211)
          ____ locations/sizes ____ elevation points ____ notes/refs
          coord check: ____ civil/soil ____ landscape

____ ____ FOUNDATION WALL AND BASEMENT WALLS 03300 (03306/03307)
          (Show walls below grade in dash line.)
          ____ elevation points
          ____ materials ____ dimensions ____ detail keys ____ notes/refs
          coord check: ____ civil/soil ____ struct

____ ____ FOOTINGS AT FOUNDATION WALLS AND BASEMENT WALLS 03300 (03305)
          ____ elevation points at bottoms of footings
          ____ materials ____ dimensions ____ detail keys ____ notes/refs
          coord check: ____ civil/soil ____ struct ____ drain

____ ____ BUILDING SLAB FOOTING LINES 03300 (03308/03309)
          ____ slab floor line
          ____ chimney footings in slab
          ____ slab footings at other concentrated loads
          ____ elevation points at bottom of footings
          ____ materials ____ dimensions ____ detail keys ____ notes/refs
          coord check: ____ civil/soil ____ struct ____ drain

EXTERIOR ELEVATIONS--SUBGRADE TO FLOOR LINE Continued

IN   OK

___ ___   DRAINPIPE AND GRAVEL BED AT FOOTINGS 02400 (02411)
          ___ elevation points
          ___ slopes
          ___ materials ___ detail keys ___ notes/refs
          coord check: ___ civil/soil ___ struct ___ site/drain

___ ___   BASEMENT WALL OPENINGS
          ___ CONCRETE 03300 (03306/03307/03316)
          ___ CONCRETE BLOCK 04200 (04229/04230)
          ___ materials ___ dimensions ___ detail keys ___ notes/refs
          coord check: ___ struct

___ ___   BASEMENT WALL AREAWAYS
          ___ materials ___ dimensions ___ detail keys ___ notes/refs
          coord check: ___ fl plan ___ cross sect

___ ___   FOUNDATION CRAWLSPACE AREAWAYS
          ___ materials ___ dimensions ___ detail keys ___ notes/refs
          coord check: ___ fl plan ___ cross sect

___ ___   GRATING COVERS FOR AREAWAYS 05500 (05530)
          ___ materials ___ dimensions ___ detail keys ___ notes/refs
          coord check: ___ fl plan ___ cross sect

___ ___   GUARDRAILS AT AREAWAYS 02440/05500 (02451/05520)
          ___ materials ___ dimensions ___ detail keys ___ notes/refs
          coord check: ___ code ___ fl plan ___ cross sect

___ ___   CRAWL SPACE VENTS/SCREENS 10200 (10200)
          ___ materials ___ dimensions ___ detail keys ___ notes/refs
          coord check: ___ code ___ fl plan ___ cross sect ___ hvac

___ ___   CRAWL SPACE ACCESS PANELS/DOORS 08300 (08305)
          ___ materials ___ dimensions ___ detail keys ___ notes/refs
          coord check: ___ fl plan ___ cross sect

___ ___   DOWNSPOUT/LEADER BOOTS 07600 (07632)
          ___ detail keys ___ notes/refs
          coord check: ___ roof ___ site/drain

___ ___   SPLASH BLOCKS 02400 (02435)
          ___ detail keys ___ notes/refs
          coord check: ___ roof ___ site/drain

EXTERIOR ELEVATIONS--SUBGRADE TO FLOOR LINE   Continued

IN   OK

___ ___   EXTERIOR WALKS
          ___   CRUSHED STONE 02500 (02511)
          ___   ASPHALTIC CONCRETE 02500 (02513)
          ___   BRICK 02500 (02514)
          ___   CONCRETE 02500 (02529)
          ___   ASPHALT 02500 (02516)
          ___   STONE 02500 (02517)
          ___   CONCRETE BLOCK/PAVERS 02500 (02518)
          ___   GRAVEL 02500 (02519)
          ___   WOOD PLANK DECK 06100 (06125)
          ___   TILE FINISH 09300 (09300)
          ___ materials ___ dimensions ___ detail keys ___ notes/refs
          ___ elevation points ___ direction of slopes
          coord check: ___ fl plan ___ site/drain

___ ___   CURBS
          ___   STONE 02500 (02524)
          ___   PRECAST CONCRETE 02500 (02526)
          ___   ASPHALT CONCRETE 02500 (02527)
          ___   CONCRETE 02500 (02528)
          ___ materials ___ dimensions ___ detail keys ___ notes/refs
          coord check: ___ fl plan

___ ___   EXTERIOR STEPS AND LANDINGS
          ___   BRICK 02500 (02514)
          ___   CONCRETE 02500 (02529)
          ___   STONE 02500 (02517)
          ___   CONCRETE BLOCK/PAVERS 02500 (02518)
          ___   WOOD PLANK DECK 06100 (06125)
          ___ materials ___ dimensions ___ detail keys ___ notes/refs
          ___ elevation points ___ slopes ___ riser number and heights
          coord check: ___ fl plan ___ site ___ site/drain

___ ___   HANDRAILS AT EXTERIOR WALKS, RAMPS AND STEPS 05500 (05520)
          ___ materials ___ dimensions ___ detail keys ___ notes/refs
          coord check: ___ code ___ fl plan ___ site

___ ___   FOOTINGS AND ROCK SUB-BASE FOR EXTERIOR SLABS 03300 (03308)
          ___ materials ___ dimensions ___ detail keys ___ notes/refs
          coord check: ___ civil/soil ___ struct ___ site

___ ___   BICYCLE AND HANDICAP RAMPS ADJACENT TO WALKWAY STEPS AND
          AT CURBS
          ___ materials ___ heights ___ detail keys ___ notes/refs
          coord check: ___ code ___ site

EXTERIOR ELEVATIONS--SUBGRADE TO FLOOR LINE Continued

IN   OK

___ ___   PLANTERS

      ___ WOOD 02440 (02447)
      ___ CONCRETE 03300 (03302)
      ___ BRICK 04200 (04203)
      ___ CONCRETE BLOCK 04200 (04228)
      ___ STONE 04400 (04400)
      ___ materials ___ dimensions ___ detail keys ___ notes/refs
      coord check: ___ landscape ___ site/drain ___ plumb

___ ___   RETAINING WALLS

      (Low height wood or brick retaining walls are usually con-
      sidered to be planter walls.)
      ___ WOOD 02440 (02447)
      ___ CONCRETE 03300 (03302)
      ___ BRICK 04200 (04203)
      ___ CONCRETE BLOCK 04200 (04228)
      ___ STONE 04400 (04400)
      ___ materials ___ heights ___ detail keys ___ notes/refs
      coord check: ___ civil/soil ___ struct ___ site/drain

___ ___   SOIL AND CRUSHED ROCK MATERIAL INDICATIONS

___ ___   DIMENSIONS OF HEIGHTS OF BUILDING ELEMENTS
      ___ footing thickness
      ___ foundation wall heights
      ___ depths of areaways
      ___ paving elevations
      ___ floor elevations
      ___ top of basement floor to top of ground floor
      ___ top of wall heights

EXTERIOR ELEVATIONS--FLOOR TO CEILING OR ROOF LINE

Most coordination checks should be made by comparing exterior elevations with floor plans and roof plans; therefore most "coord check"
notes are omitted from the following portions of the exterior elevations checklist. Only those coordination checks which might not be
also found on the floor plans or roof plan are included in this list.

IN   OK

____ ____ ADJACENT OR ATTACHED FENCES AND GATES   02440
           ____ CHAIN LINK 02440 (02444)
           ____ WIRE 02440 (02445)
           ____ WOOD 02440 (02446)
           ____ METAL 02440 (02447)
           ____ materials ____ heights ____ detail keys ____ notes/refs
           coord check: ____ site

____ ____ ADJACENT OR ATTACHED YARD WALLS
           ____ CONCRETE 03300 (03300)
           ____ BRICK 04200 (04210)
           ____ CONCRETE BLOCK 04200 (04220)
           ____ STONE 04400 (04400)
           ____ materials ____ heights ____ detail keys ____ notes/refs
           coord check: ____ site

____ ____ CONSTRUCTION JOINTS
           (Minor joints are normally not shown but are indicated in de-
           tails and/or notation.)
           ____ CONTROL JOINTS IN CONCRETE WALLS 03250 (03251)
           ____ CONTROL JOINTS IN MASONRY SPANDRELS OVER OPENINGS
                04150 (04180)
           ____ PLYWOOD SIDING MOVEMENT JOINTS (1/4" BETWEEN PANELS)
                07400 (07461)
           ____ METAL EXTERIOR EXPANSION JOINTS 05800 (05802)
           ____ locations ____ detail keys ____ notes/refs
           coord check: ____ specs ____ struct

____ ____ WEEP HOLES
           (Normally indicated in details and general notes rather
           than in the broadscope Exterior Elevations.)
           ____ RETAINING WALLS 02400 (02415)
           ____ BRICK CAVITY WALLS 04200 (04210)
           ____ CONCRETE BLOCK CAVITY WALLS 04200 (04220)
           ____ MASONRY VENEER 04200 (04215)
           ____ GLAZED METAL CURTAIN WALLS 08900 (08900)
           ____ heights/spacings ____ detail keys ____ notes/refs

____ ____ EXTERIOR-MOUNTED HVAC ENCLOSURES 05500 (05551)
           ____ heights ____ detail keys ____ notes/refs
           coord check: ____ code ____ hvac ____ wall anch ____ elec

EXTERIOR ELEVATIONS--FLOOR TO CEILING OR ROOF LINE Continued

IN   OK

___ ___   EXTERIOR LANDING OR STOOP PAVING
          (Top of exterior landing 3" below door thresholds.)
          ___ BRICK PAVING 02500 (02514)
          ___ STONE PAVING 02500 (02517)
          ___ CONCRETE MASONRY PAVING 02400 (02518)
          ___ CONCRETE PAVING 02500 (02529)
          ___ WOOD DECK 06100 (06125)
          ___ materials ___ dimensions ___ detail keys ___ notes/refs
          ___ elevation points ___ slopes
          coord check: ___ site

___ ___   HANDRAILS AT EXTERIOR STAIR LANDINGS OR STOOPS 05500
          (05520/05521)
          ___ materials ___ dimensions ___ detail keys ___ notes/refs
          coord check: ___ slab/wall anch

___ ___   DECK, PORCH, AND BALCONY RAILINGS OR WALLS
          (Newels or horizontal members spaced at 9" maximum.)
          ___ BRICK 04200 (04210)
          ___ CONCRETE BLOCK 04200 (04220)
          ___ METAL 05500/05700 (05520/05720)
          ___ WOOD 06400 (06440)
          ___ CHAIN LINK/WIRE 04200 (02444/02445)
          ___ materials ___ dimensions ___ detail keys ___ notes/refs
          coord check: ___ slab/wall anch

___ ___   METERS
          ___ GAS 15050 (15182)
          ___ ELECTRIC 16400 (16430)
          ___ heights ___ notes/refs
          coord check: ___ util ___ site ___ wall anch

___ ___   POSTS, COLUMNS, AND PILASTERS
          ___ CONCRETE 03300 (03317)
          ___ PRECAST CONCRETE 03400 (03410)
          ___ REINFORCED BRICK 04200 (04216)
          ___ REINFORCED CONCRETE BLOCK 04200 (04230)
          ___ STEEL WF 05100 (05120)
          ___ TUBULAR STEEL 05100 (05122)
          ___ WOOD 06100 (06101 to 06104)
          ___ HEAVY TIMBER 06130 (06132/06133)
          ___ materials ___ heights ___ detail keys ___ notes/refs
          coord check: ___ struct ___ site

___ ___   PARKING GUARDRAILS 02440 (02451)
          ___ materials ___ dimensions ___ detail keys ___ notes/refs
          coord check: ___ site ___ cross sect

EXTERIOR ELEVATIONS--FLOOR TO CEILING OR ROOF LINE Continued

IN   OK

___ ___   PARKING BUMPERS 02440 (02456)
          ___ materials ___ dimensions ___ detail keys ___ notes/refs
          coord check: ___ site ___ slab/wall anch

___ ___   CORNER GUARDS 10260 (10260)
          ___ materials ___ heights ___ detail keys ___ notes/refs
          coord check: ___ wall anch

___ ___   LOADING DOCK 11160 (11160)
          ___ materials ___ dimensions ___ detail keys ___ notes/refs
          coord check: ___ site ___ cross sect ___ wall anch ___ elec

___ ___   DOCK BUMPERS 11160 (11165)
          ___ materials ___ detail keys ___ notes/refs
          coord check: ___ wall anch

___ ___   LOADING DOCK SHELTER 11160 (11164)
          (Canopy height clearance for trucks.)
          ___ materials ___ heights ___ detail keys ___ notes/refs
          coord check: ___ roof ___ cross sect ___ wall anch ___ elec

___ ___   EXTERIOR FINISH CARPENTRY 06200 (06200)
          ___ dimensions/spacings ___ detail keys ___ notes/refs
          coord check: ___ millwork schedule

___ ___   DOWNSPOUTS 07600 (07632)
          ___ gutters
          ___ leaders
          ___ leader connection to wall
          ___ materials ___ dimensions ___ detail keys ___ notes/refs
          coord check: ___ roof ___ site/drain ___ wall anch

___ ___   HOSE BIBBS/WALL HYDRANTS 15050 (15109)
          (Shown only if important in relationship to other elements.)
          ___ heights ___ notes/refs
          coord check: ___ plumb ___ wall anch ___ drain

___ ___   STANDPIPES 15500 (15530)
          (Siamese connections for Fire Department and identifying signs.)
          ___ locations ___ detail keys ___ notes/refs
          coord check: ___ code ___ plumb ___ wall anch

___ ___   INTEGRATED STOREFRONT SYSTEM 08400 (08400)
          ___ materials ___ heights ___ detail keys ___ notes/refs
          coord check: ___ sched

EXTERIOR ELEVATIONS--FLOOR TO CEILING OR ROOF LINE Continued

IN   OK

___ ___   CAULKING AT DOOR AND WINDOW FRAMES 07900 (07900)
          (Caulking is particularly required in masonry walls.)
          ___ detail keys ___ notes/refs
          coord check: ___ specs

___ ___   DOOR AND WINDOW FLASHING 07600 (07620 to 07626)
          ___ detail keys ___ notes/refs
          coord check: ___ specs

___ ___   DOORS AND WINDOWS
          (Door and window identification and schedule keys are shown on
          plan; detail keys are to be shown on the door and window frame
          schedules. Door and window detail keys are sometimes also
          added to the plan and elevation drawings in special cases, to
          call attention to exceptional conditions.)
          ___ sills
          ___ trim
          ___ muntins
          ___ mullions
          ___ direction of swing, direction of slide, swing of hopper
              units may be shown in special cases
          ___ heights ___ detail keys ___ notes/refs
          coord check: ___ schedules

___ ___   SHUTTERS
          ___ METAL 10240 (10245)
          ___ WOOD 06200 (06235)
          ___ materials ___ heights ___ detail keys ___ notes/refs
          coord check: ___ wall anch

___ ___   GRILLES AT WINDOWS 10240 (10241)
          (Used mainly where windows are accessible from exterior
          walkways or stairs.)
          ___ materials ___ heights ___ detail keys ___ notes/refs
          coord check: ___ wall anch ___ window sched

___ ___   WIRE MESH WINDOW GUARDS 10240 (10242)
          ___ fixed ___ operable
          ___ materials ___ dimensions ___ detail keys ___ notes/refs
          coord check: ___ wall anch ___ window sched

___ ___   SECURITY WINDOWS 08650 (08651)
          ___ materials ___ heights ___ detail keys ___ notes/refs
          coord check: ___ window sched

EXTERIOR ELEVATIONS--FLOOR TO CEILING OR ROOF LINE Continued

IN   OK

___ ___ GLAZING
(Glass type should be identified in window schedule but may be
noted in plans or elevations in drawings for smaller buildings.)

___   DOUBLE GLAZING 08800 (08802)
___   INSULATING GLASS 08800 (08823)
___   LAMINATED SAFETY GLASS 08800 (08822)
___   OBSCURE GLASS/ROUGH AND FIGURED 08800 (08815)
___   PLATE/FLOAT GLASS 08800 (08811)
___   PLASTIC GLAZING 08600/08800 (08620/08840)
___   PLASTIC INSULATING GLAZING 08800 (08845)
___   SPANDREL GLASS 08800 (08817)
___   STAINED GLASS 12100 (12170)
___   TEMPERED GLASS 08800 (08813)
___   materials ___   heights ___   detail keys ___   notes/refs
coord check: ___   specs ___   window sched

___ ___ AIR INTAKE OR VENT LOUVERS 10200 (10200)
___   materials ___   heights ___   detail keys ___   notes/refs
coord check: ___   hvac

___ ___ AIR INTAKE OR VENT GRILLES AND SCREENS 10200 (10240)
___   materials ___   heights ___   detail keys ___   notes/refs
coord check: ___   hvac

___ ___ BUILDING NAME AND ADDRESS PLAQUES 10400 (10420)
___   materials ___   location ___   detail keys ___   notes/refs
coord check: ___   site ___   elec

___ ___ ARCHITECT'S PLAQUE 10400 (10420)
___   materials ___   location ___   detail keys ___   notes/refs
coord check: ___   site

___ ___ EXTERIOR-MOUNTED FIRE ALARMS 16700 (16721)
___   heights ___   detail keys ___   notes/refs
coord check: ___   code ___   elec

___ ___ EXTERIOR-MOUNTED BURGLAR ALARMS 16700 (16727)
___   heights ___   detail keys ___   notes/refs
coord check: ___   elec

___ ___ WALL-MOUNTED FLAGPOLES 10350 (10354)
___   heights ___   detail keys ___   notes/refs
coord check: ___   wall anch

___ ___ EXTERIOR BUILDING LIGHTING 16500 (16520)
___   locations ___   notes/refs
coord check: ___   site ___   elec

EXTERIOR ELEVATIONS--FLOOR TO CEILING OR ROOF LINE Continued

IN   OK

___ ___   WALL-MOUNTED SIGNS 10400 (10440)
            ___ materials ___ dimensions ___ detail keys ___ notes/refs
            coord check: ___ wall anch ___ elec

___ ___   NIGHT DEPOSITORY SLOTS AND BOX 11020 (11026)
            ___ heights ___ detail keys ___ notes/refs
            coord check: ___ site ___ elec

___ ___   WASTE HANDLING EQUIPMENT 11170 (11170)
            ___ locations ___ notes/refs
            coord check: ___ site

___ ___   TRASH/WASTE HANDLING EQUIPMENT ENCLOSURES
            ___ CHAIN LINK FENCE 02400 (02444)
            ___ WIRE FENCE 02400 (02445)
            ___ WOOD 02400 (02446)
            ___ BRICK 04200 (04210)
            ___ CONCRETE BLOCK 04200 (04220)
            ___ materials ___ dimensions ___ detail keys ___ notes/refs
            coord check: ___ site ___ elec

___ ___   THRU-WALL FLASHING 07600 (07620 to 07626)
            ___ detail keys ___ notes/refs
            coord check: ___ specs

___ ___   DRIPS AT UNDERSIDE EDGE OF CANTILEVERED BALCONIES AND WALL
            PROJECTIONS
            ___ locations ___ detail keys ___ notes/refs
            coord check: ___ struct

___ ___   MARQUEES 10530 (10533)
            ___ materials ___ dimensions ___ detail keys ___ notes/refs
            coord check: ___ struct ___ roof ___ cross sect
                         ___ wall anch

___ ___   AWNINGS 10530 (10535)
            ___ materials ___ dimensions ___ detail keys ___ notes/refs
            coord check: ___ wall anch

___ ___   CANOPIES 10530 (10531)
            ___ scuppers/rain water leaders
            ___ materials ___ dimensions ___ detail keys ___ notes/refs
            coord check: ___ struct ___ roof ___ cross sect
                         ___ wall anch

___ ___   SUN SCREENS 10700 (10700)
            ___ materials ___ dimensions ___ detail keys ___ notes/refs
            coord check: ___ struct ___ wall anch

EXTERIOR ELEVATIONS--FLOOR TO CEILING OR ROOF LINE Continued

IN   OK

___ ___ EXTERIOR WALLS AND WALL FINISHES

       ___ ADOBE 04200 (04212)

       ___ BRICK 04200 (04210)

       ___ BRICK CAVITY WALL 04200 (04214)

       ___ BRICK VENEER 04200 (04215)

       ___ CONCRETE BLOCK, REINFORCED 04200 (04230)

       ___ CONCRETE, CAST-IN-PLACE 03300 (03316)

       ___ CONCRETE, PRECAST 03400 (03450)

       ___ CONCRETE, PRECAST PANELS 03400 (03411)

       ___ CONCRETE, TILT-UP 03400 (03430)

       ___ GLAZED CURTAIN WALLS 08900 (08900)

       ___ ROUGH STONE 04400 (04410)

       ___ CUT STONE 04400 (04420)

       ___ FLAGSTONE 04400 (04440)

       ___ MARBLE VENEER 04400 (04451)

       ___ NATURAL STONE VENEER 04400 (04450)

       ___ WOOD FRAMING AND SHEATHING 06100 (06110)

       ___ PLYWOOD SIDING 07400 (07465)

       ___ WOOD SIDING 07400 (07461)

       ___ METAL SIDING 07400 (07411)

       ___ STUCCO 09200 (09230)

       ___ wall material indications, textures, and patterns
       ___ material ___ heights ___ detail keys ___ notes/refs
coord check: ___ cross sect ___ wall sect

EXTERIOR ELEVATIONS--CEILING LINE TO ROOF

IN   OK

___ ___ FASCIAS
            ___ CONCRETE, CAST-IN-PLACE 03300 (03330)
            ___ CONCRETE, PRECAST 03400 (03450)
            ___ TERRA COTTA 04200 (04251)
            ___ METAL 05700 (05730)
            ___ WOOD 06200 (06260)
            ___ materials ___ dimensions ___ detail keys ___ notes/refs
         coord check: ___ ref clg ___ cross sect

___ ___ EXTERIOR SOFFITS
            ___ METAL 05700 (05730)
            ___ WOOD SIDING 07400 (07460)
            ___ STUCCO 09200 (09230)
            ___ exterior soffit lines
            ___ construction and control joints
            ___ materials ___ dimensions ___ detail keys ___ notes/refs
         coord check: ___ ref clg ___ cross sect

___ ___ EAVE SOFFIT VENTS 10200/10240 (10200/10240)
            ___ materials ___ dimensions ___ detail keys ___ notes/refs
         coord check: ___ ref clg ___ hvac

___ ___ RIDGE VENTS 07600 (07630)
            ___ materials ___ dimensions ___ detail keys ___ notes/refs
         coord check: ___ roof ___ hvac

___ ___ ATTIC VENTS 10200/10240 (10200/10240)
            ___ materials ___ dimensions ___ detail keys ___ notes/refs
         coord check: ___ roof ___ hvac

___ ___ GRAVEL STOPS 07600 (07660)
            ___ materials ___ dimensions ___ detail keys ___ notes/refs
         coord check: ___ specs ___ roof

___ ___ CAP FLASHING 07600 (07603)
            ___ materials ___ dimensions ___ detail keys ___ notes/refs
         coord check: ___ specs ___ roof

___ ___ GUTTERS 07600 (07631)
            ___ materials ___ dimensions ___ detail keys ___ notes/refs
         coord check: ___ roof ___ site/drain ___ wall anch

___ ___ RAIN DEFLECTORS 07600 (07634)
            ___ materials ___ dimensions ___ detail keys ___ notes/refs
         coord check: ___ roof ___ site/drain

EXTERIOR ELEVATIONS--CEILING LINE TO ROOF   Continued

IN   OK

___ ___   DOWNSPOUTS 07600 (07632)
          ___ materials ___ dimensions ___ detail keys ___ notes/refs
          coord check: ___ roof ___ site/drain ___ wall anch

___ ___   RAIN DOWNSPOUT LEADERS AND LEADER STRAPS 07600 (07632)
          ___ materials ___ dimensions ___ detail keys ___ notes/refs
          coord check: ___ site/drain ___ wall anch

___ ___   SCUPPERS 07600 (07633)
          ___ materials ___ dimensions ___ detail keys ___ notes/refs
          coord check: ___ roof ___ site/drain ___ wall anch

___ ___   EAVE SNOW GUARDS 07600 (07635)
          ___ materials ___ dimensions ___ detail keys ___ notes/refs
          coord check: ___ roof

___ ___   PARAPETS
          ___ CONCRETE, CAST-IN-PLACE 03300 (03330)
          ___ CONCRETE, PRECAST 03400 (03450)
          ___ BRICK 04200 (04210)
          ___ CONCRETE BLOCK 04200 (04220)
          ___ METAL FRAME 05100 (05100/05400)
          ___ WOOD FRAME 06100 (06168)
          ___ materials ___ dimensions ___ detail keys ___ notes/refs
          coord check: ___ struct ___ roof ___ cross sect
          ___ wall sect

___ ___   PARAPET COPINGS
          (Parapet cap slope inward toward roof.)
          ___ MASONRY 04200 (04200)
          ___ STONE 04400 (04420)
          ___ METAL 07600 (07665)
          ___ materials ___ dimensions ___ detail keys ___ notes/refs
          coord check: ___ roof ___ wall sect

___ ___   PARAPET EXPANSION JOINTS 05800 (05802)
          ___ locations ___ detail keys ___ notes/refs
          coord check: ___ specs ___ wall sect

___ ___   RAILINGS 05500 (05520/05521)
          ___ materials ___ dimensions ___ detail keys ___ notes/refs
          coord check: ___ code ___ struct ___ roof/wall anch
          ___ wall sect

___ ___   ROOF LADDERS 05500 (05517)
          ___ materials ___ dimensions ___ detail keys ___ notes/refs
          coord check: ___ struct ___ roof/wall anch

EXTERIOR ELEVATIONS--CEILING LINE TO ROOF Continued

IN   OK

____ ____ FINISH ROOFING MATERIALS
            ___ ASPHALT SHINGLES 07300 (07311)
            ___ WOOD SHINGLES/SHAKES 07300 (07313)
            ___ SLATE SHINGLES 07300 (07314)
            ___ METAL SHINGLES 07300 (07316)
            ___ CLAY TILES 07300 (07321)
            ___ CONCRETE TILES 07300 (07322)
            ___ PREFORMED METAL 07400 (07412)
            ___ BUILT-UP ROOF 07500 (07510)
            ___ MEMBRANE ROOF 07500 (07550 to 07560)
            ___ SHEET METAL 07600 (07610)
            ___ detail keys ___ notes/refs
            coord check: ___ specs ___ roof ___ cross sect

____ ____ SKYLIGHTS 07800 (07810)
            ___ materials ___ dimensions ___ detail keys ___ notes/refs
            coord check: ___ roof ___ cross sect

____ ____ MECHANICAL EQUIPMENT ENCLOSURE
            ___ materials ___ dimensions ___ detail keys ___ notes/refs
            coord check: ___ roof ___ hvac

____ ____ COOLING TOWERS 15650 (15650)
            ___ materials ___ dimensions ___ detail keys ___ notes/refs
            coord check: ___ roof ___ hvac

____ ____ COOLING TOWER PENTHOUSE
            ___ materials ___ dimensions ___ detail keys ___ notes/refs
            coord check: ___ roof ___ hvac

____ ____ SOLAR HEAT COLLECTION PANELS 13980 (13980)
            ___ materials ___ dimensions ___ detail keys ___ notes/refs
            coord check: ___ struct ___ roof ___ roof anch ___ hvac
                  ___ cross sect

____ ____ SOLAR WATER HEATERS 13980/15400 (13980/15431)
            ___ materials ___ dimensions ___ detail keys ___ notes/refs
            coord check: ___ struct ___ roof ___ roof anch ___ hvac
                  ___ cross sect

____ ____ WATER TANKS 13400/15400 (13410/15400)
            ___ materials ___ dimensions ___ detail keys ___ notes/refs
            coord check: ___ roof ___ struct ___ plumb

____ ____ WATER TANK ENCLOSURE
            ___ materials ___ dimensions ___ detail keys ___ notes/refs
            coord check: ___ roof

EXTERIOR ELEVATIONS--CEILING LINE TO ROOF Continued

IN   OK

___ ___   STAIR BULKHEADS
          ___ materials ___ dimensions ___ detail keys ___ notes/refs
          coord check: ___ stair pl/sect ___ roof ___ cross sect

___ ___   ELEVATOR PENTHOUSE/MACHINE ROOM 14200 (14200)
          ___ materials ___ dimensions ___ detail keys ___ notes/refs
          coord check: ___ elev pl/sect ___ roof ___ cross sect

___ ___   CHIMNEYS
          ___ MASONRY 04200 (04210)
          ___ PREFAB 10300 (10300)
          ___ flues
          ___ spark arrestors
          ___ coping caps
          ___ chimney coping block or cement wash slope toward flue
          ___ materials ___ dimensions ___ detail keys ___ notes/refs
          coord check: ___ code ___ struct ___ hvac ___ cross sect

___ ___   CHIMNEY FLASHING 07600 (07608)
          ___ saddle
          ___ cricket
          ___ materials ___ dimensions ___ detail keys ___ notes/refs
          coord check: ___ specs

___ ___   ROOF ANTENNAS
          ___ TV TOWER MASTER ANTENNA 16700 (06781)
          ___ SATELLITE DISH ANTENNA 11800 (11800)
          ___ BROADCAST ANTENNA 16700 (16790)
          ___ locations ___ detail keys ___ notes/refs
          coord check: ___ code ___ struct ___ roof anch ___ elec

___ ___   GUY WIRE ANCHORS FOR TV, FM, OR SHORTWAVE ANTENNAS
          07800 (07871)
          ___ detail keys ___ notes/refs
          coord check: ___ roof anch

___ ___   FLAGPOLES 10350 (10360)
          ___ locations/heights ___ detail keys ___ notes/refs
          coord check: ___ struct ___ roof ___ roof anch ___ elec

___ ___   LIGHTNING RODS 16600 (16601)
          ___ detail keys ___ notes/refs
          coord check: ___ roof ___ roof anch ___ elec

___ ___   WEATHER VANES 05700 (05745)
          ___ detail keys ___ notes/refs
          coord check: ___ roof ___ roof anch

EXTERIOR ELEVATIONS--CEILING LINE TO ROOF Continued

IN   OK

___ ___   OVERHEAD CABLE PERISCOPE ENTRY HEADS 16400 (16401/16420)
          ___ detail keys ___ notes/refs
          coord check: ___ util ___ roof/wall anch

___ ___   ROOF-MOUNTED SIGNS 10400 (10430/10440)
          ___ materials ___ dimensions ___ detail keys ___ notes/refs
          coord check: ___ code ___ struct ___ roof anch ___ elec

___ ___   PREFABRICATED ROOF SPECIALTIES
          ___ STEEPLES 10340 (10341)
          ___ SPIRES 10340 (10342)
          ___ CUPOLAS 10340 (10343)
          ___ materials ___ dimensions ___ detail keys ___ notes/refs
          coord check: ___ struct ___ roof ___ roof anch
                        ___ cross sect

___ ___   ROOFING MATERIALS INDICATIONS

___ ___   DIMENSIONS
          ___ roof slopes in inches per foot
          ___ eave overhang
          ___ depth of fascia
          ___ height of parapet
          ___ height of equipment enclosures
          ___ floor-to-floor heights
          ___ window, door, opening head heights from floor line
          ___ floor-to-ceiling heights
          ___ note whether vertical dimensions are to finish surfaces,
              subflooring, or framing
          ___ note whether opening dimensions are rough or finish

6.0

CHAPTER SIX--BUILDING CROSS SECTIONS   6.0 - 6.8

BUILDING CROSS SECTIONS--INTRODUCTION

Building cross sections are usually the most overdrawn of any drawings
in a working drawing set.

Their primary purpose is to show level-to-level heights, the overall
structural/construction system, and to identify tricky areas such as
junctures and changes in floor, ceiling and roof construction.

Floor, wall, ceiling and roof construction need only be drawn schemat-
ically. Add detail bubbles and numbers to reference the more specific, larger-scale sections and details.

ITEMS THAT SHOULD BE AVOIDED ON CROSS SECTION DRAWINGS

____ Don't show interior elevation drawings of the "back walls" of a
cross section drawing. That will only duplicate or contradict
other drawings such as the floor plans, interior elevations and
exterior elevations. Although "back walls" make the drawing look
more complete, they usually will serve no real useful purpose for
the contractor. The exception is when you have only one space or
a single line of rooms in a building and the cross section does
double duty as the interior elevation sheet.

____ If you show doors or windows, don't show door or window symbols.
That will also either duplicate or contradict the floor plans.

____ Don't indicate interior finishes. That's the province of floor
plans, interior elevations, and the finish schedule.

____ Don't show interior furnishings and fixtures. That's another
common source of duplication or error. Show only those special
fixtures or equipment, if any, that affect the overall structure.

COORDINATION

____ The cross section should be derived directly from the exterior
elevation drawings, which themselves have been derived directly
from the floor plans. Then double check the accuracy of the
elevations by overlaying the cross sections on the floor plans.

____ The necessity to check coordination of the cross sections with the
floor plans is assumed in this list and not cited in the "coord
check" notes. The necessity to check coordination of sections with
specifications is also assumed, as it is in other chapters of the
checklist, but some special cases are added to the "coord check"
lists as extra reminders.

BUILDING CROSS SECTIONS--INTRODUCTION Continued

ITEMS SUITED TO SYSTEMS DRAFTING, PASTE-UP, AND OVERLAY

____ If presentation drawings include cross sections, have the sections show linework only. Show rendering entourage, titles, design options, phased construction, etc. only on overlays. Make prints of those base sheet/overlay combinations for presentation purposes. This process saves the uncluttered cross section drawing for easy revision and possible direct reuse as a working drawing sheet.

____ Use appropriate exterior elevation drawings as base sheets or as background sheets for your cross sections instead of measuring and drawing wall and floor sections from scratch. Overlay cross section drawings directly on floor plans to identify any special interior features that should be included in the sections.

____ In some cases the exterior elevations can be reversed, screen printed, and used as a subdued background for the solid line section drawings. In this instance it's OK to show "back walls" since they're not being drawn as a separate process.

____ If the vertical walls at each end of the building are identical or similar to one another, draw one wall section and make contact print copies both "right reading" and "reverse" for paste-up. Paste them up as the two ends of each building cross section and add connective floor, ceiling and roof lines.

____ If you have drawn or sketched complete, large-scale wall sections previously, and if you're using photo reduction techniques, you can make reduced-sized copies both "right read" and "reverse" for paste-up. Complete the paste-up with connective lines as described above.

____ You can use "ruby red" litho tape or graphic tape to do solid, undetailed strips of wall, partition, slab, and roof construction. Use keynotes and/or section reference bubbles to identify construction of each component.

____ Provide consultants with base sheets or background sheets of cross sections whenever their work is also shown in such sections. They won't have to redraw your building, and everyone's work will remain 100% graphically coordinated.

____ Notes for cross sections are highly repetitive, so you can readily use one keynote strip and bubble reference all notation in the drawing to a notation legend.

____ In lieu of keynoting, you can create one or more strips of notes and copy them as stickybacks or translucent paste-ups to add on to each cross section.

BUILDING CROSS SECTIONS--REFERENCE INFORMATION

IN   OK

___ ___   KEY PLAN IDENTIFICATION OF CROSS SECTION CUT POINTS
            coord check: ___ ext elev

___ ___   EXISTING AND NEW FINISH GRADE LINES WITH ELEVATIONS
            coord check: ___ ext elev ___ civil ___ site

___ ___   HEIGHTS AND ELEVATION POINTS
            ___ finish floor to finish floor or subfloor to subfloor
            ___ floor or subfloor to finish ceiling
            ___ floor or subfloor to underside of beams, headers and
                lintels
            ___ upper floor to roof
            coord check: ___ struct ___ ext elev ___ wall sect

___ ___   NOTE WHETHER DIMENSIONS ARE TO FINISH SURFACES, ROUGH
            SURFACES OR STRUCTURE

BUILDING CROSS SECTIONS--CONSTRUCTION COMPONENTS
SUBGRADE THROUGH GROUND FLOOR

Most items are assumed to require cross checking with floor plans and
exterior elevations and so are not cited for "coord check" with those
drawings on every listing.

CSI coordination numbers are not included in this list. Those numbers
can be found linked to their building components in other chapters and
aren't helpful in checklisting this generalized type of drawing.

IN   OK

____ ____ FOOTINGS AND FOUNDATION WALLS
            ____ materials ____ dimensions ____ detail keys ____ notes/refs
            coord check: ____ struct ____ civil

____ ____ FOUNDATION DRAINS
            ____ drain tiles
            ____ crushed rock drain tile bed
            ____ roof drain connections to storm sewer
            ____ materials ____ dimensions ____ detail keys ____ notes/refs
            coord check: ____ struct ____ site/drain

____ ____ BASEMENT AREAWAYS
            ____ areaway wall and footing
            ____ drain
            ____ window or hatch section
            ____ materials ____ dimensions ____ detail keys ____ notes/refs
            coord check: ____ struct ____ site/drain

____ ____ PIPES AND SLEEVES THAT PENETRATE BASEMENT WALL
            ____ heights/sizes ____ detail keys ____ notes/refs
            coord check: ____ struct ____ util ____ plumb ____ hvac
                         ____ elec

____ ____ ADJACENT PAVING AND WALKWAYS
            ____ slope away from building
            ____ slopes to drains
            ____ materials ____ dimensions ____ detail keys ____ notes/refs
            coord check: ____ site/drain ____ ext elev

____ ____ ADJACENT STOOPS, PLATFORMS, AND LANDINGS
            ____ materials ____ dimensions ____ detail keys ____ notes/refs
            coord check: ____ site ____ ext elev

____ ____ EXTERIOR SLAB FOOTINGS OR FROST CURBS
            ____ tamped fill
            ____ sand and gravel fill
            ____ vapor barrier
            ____ reinforcing
            ____ materials ____ dimensions ____ detail keys ____ notes/refs
            coord check: ____ struct ____ site

BUILDING CROSS SECTIONS--CONSTRUCTION COMPONENTS
GROUND FLOOR THROUGH ROOF

IN   OK

___ ___   FLOOR CONSTRUCTION
          ___ framing
          ___ floor slabs and deck
          ___ subflooring and floor topping
          ___ floor waterproofing at wet rooms
          ___ depressed slabs for varied finish flooring thicknesses
          ___ curbs
          ___ pedestals
          ___ trenches
          ___ pits and guardrails
          ___ cantilevered slabs
          ___ materials ___ dimensions ___ detail keys ___ notes/refs
          coord check: ___ struct

___ ___   EXTERIOR WALLS
          ___ types (See Floor Plans)
          ___ ledgers
          ___ spandrel beams
          ___ spandrel angles
          ___ materials ___ dimensions ___ detail keys ___ notes/refs
          coord check: ___ struct ___ ext elev

___ ___   DOOR AND WINDOW OPENINGS
          ___ sills and saddles
          ___ head framing
          ___ stools and aprons
          ___ materials ___ dimensions ___ detail keys ___ notes/refs
          coord check: ___ struct ___ ext elev

___ ___   GIRDERS, BEAMS, AND JOISTS
          ___ hangers
          ___ anchors
          ___ stirrups
          ___ pockets
          ___ ledgers
          ___ bearing plates
          ___ bridging and blocking
          ___ materials ___ dimensions ___ detail keys ___ notes/refs
          coord check: ___ struct ___ hvac

___ ___   SUSPENDED MECHANICAL WORK
          ___ materials ___ dimensions ___ detail keys ___ notes/refs
          coord check: ___ struct ___ slab anch ___ hvac

BUILDING CROSS SECTIONS--CONSTRUCTION COMPONENTS
GROUND FLOOR THROUGH ROOF Continued

IN   OK

____ ____ INTERIOR WALLS AND CEILINGS
       ____ light coves
       ____ coffers
       ____ valances
       ____ vapor barriers
       ____ rigid or batt terminal insulation
       ____ fireproof construction
       ____ soundproofing
       ____ acoustical treatments
       ____ wainscots
       ____ finishes
       ____ materials ____ dimensions ____ detail keys ____ notes/refs
       coord check: ____ struct ____ hvac ____ plumb ____ elec
              ____ ref clg ____ fin sched

____ ____ SUSPENDED CEILINGS
       ____ main tees, cross tees, and hangers
       ____ ceiling-mounted equipment
       ____ ceiling or attic barriers
       ____ coffers
       ____ materials ____ dimensions ____ detail keys ____ notes/refs
       coord check: ____ struct ____ hvac ____ plumb ____ elec
              ____ ref clg ____ fin sched

____ ____ COLUMNS AND POSTS
       ____ base plates
       ____ piers
       ____ pedestals
       ____ fireproofing
       ____ column caps
       ____ drop panels
       ____ column splices
       ____ stiffeners
       ____ wind bracing
       ____ cross ties
       ____ materials ____ dimensions ____ detail keys ____ notes/refs
       coord check: ____ struct ____ int elevs

____ ____ SUSPENDED HEAVY EQUIPMENT
       ____ hoists/cranes
       ____ fixtures/hvac equipment
       ____ materials ____ dimensions ____ detail keys ____ notes/refs
       coord check: ____ struct ____ slab anch ____ mech ____ elec

____ ____ SUSPENDED OR CANTILEVERED INTERIOR BALCONIES
       ____ materials ____ dimensions ____ detail keys ____ notes/refs
       coord check: ____ struct ____ mech

BUILDING CROSS SECTIONS--CONSTRUCTION COMPONENTS, ROOF

For other more specialized components that might be included in
cross sections, see Chapter Four, Roof Plans.

IN   OK

___ ___   PARAPETS
          ___ caps
          ___ overflows
          ___ materials ___ dimensions ___ detail keys ___ notes/refs
          coord check: ___ wall sect ___ roof ___ ext elev

___ ___   TRUSSES
          ___ truss splices
          ___ sway bracing
          ___ sag rods
          ___ purlins
          ___ materials ___ dimensions ___ detail keys ___ notes/refs
          coord check: ___ struct ___ roof

___ ___   OVERHANGS
          ___ fascia
          ___ soffit
          ___ soffit vents
          ___ trim
          ___ expansion joints
          ___ materials ___ dimensions ___ detail keys ___ notes/refs
          coord check: ___ struct ___ roof ___ ext elev

___ ___   ROOF DECKING OR SHEATHING
          ___ finish roofing materials
          ___ roof expansion joints
          ___ slopes
          ___ materials ___ dimensions ___ detail keys ___ notes/refs
          coord check: ___ specs ___ roof

___ ___   ROOF APPURTENANCES
          ___ penthouse
          ___ stair bulkhead
          ___ elevator bulkhead
          ___ mechanical equipment
          ___ water tower
          ___ thru-roof vent pipes and flues
          ___ curbs
          ___ anchors
          ___ pitch pockets
          ___ snow melting equipment
          ___ railings
          ___ solar panels
          ___ materials ___ dimensions ___ detail keys ___ notes/refs
          coord check: ___ struct ___ roof ___ mech ___ ext elev

BUILDING CROSS SECTIONS--CONSTRUCTION COMPONENTS, ROOF   Continued

IN   OK

___ ___   THRU-BUILDING SHAFTS
          ___ elevator shaft, hoist, and pit
          ___ escalator
          ___ stairs/smoke towers
          ___ trash chute
          ___ conveyors
          ___ plumbing chases
          ___ hvac chases
          ___ electrical chases
          ___ interior rain water leaders
          ___ materials ___ dimensions ___ detail keys ___ notes/refs
          coord check: ___ struct ___ elevator pl/sect ___ stair pl/sect
                   ___ hvac ___ plumb ___ elec

___ ___   SKYLIGHTS
          ___ light shafts
          ___ condensation collectors
          ___ mesh guards
          ___ materials ___ dimensions ___ detail keys ___ notes/refs
          coord check: ___ struct ___ roof

CHAPTER SEVEN--REFLECTED CEILING PLANS   7.0 - 7.10

REFLECTED CEILING PLANS--INTRODUCTION

Reflected ceiling plans serve two main purposes:

1) They show the designer's intent regarding the appearance of ceiling
    patterns and the placement of fixtures and equipment.

2) They provide base sheet or background sheet information for the
    electrical, communications, and mechanical consultants to work from
    and coordinate with one another.

Other drawings that may be derived from the architectural reflected
ceiling plans include lighting and electrical power; communications;
HVAC ceiling vents, diffusers, heaters, etc.; fire sprinklers; and
special acoustical, fire barrier and thermal insulation treatments.

ITEMS THAT SHOULD BE AVOIDED ON REFLECTED CEILING PLANS

____ The main source of overdrawing reflected ceiling plans is non-use
      of previously drawn floor plans as base sheets. In traditional
      practice, drafters draw all the walls and relevant floor plan items
      from scratch and add the reflected ceiling grid. This virtually
      assures error and quick obsolescence as drafters make floor plan
      changes and fail to keep them up to date on the ceiling drawings.

      Those errors and omissions are compounded when changes not caught
      on the reflected ceiling plans are similarly not picked up in the
      drawings by varied related consultants. Besides avoiding the re-
      dundant drawing/redrawing of floor plans, using overlays virtually
      guarantees 100% ongoing coordination between the work of all con-
      sultants and trades.

____ It's not necessary to draw suspended ceiling tile grids by hand.
      See the Systems Drafting section on page 7.3.

REFLECTED CEILING PLANS--INTRODUCTION   Continued

COORDINATION

____ The reflected ceiling plans should be derived directly from the
floor plans by means of overlay drafting or by use of reproducible
background sheets. This assures an exact, one-to-one correlation
between ceiling plans and floor plans.

____ Periodically check the reflected ceiling plans against updated
floor plans by direct overlay comparison on a light table. That's
the only way to guarantee perfect accuracy in floor plan/ceiling
coordination.

____ All related consultants' drawings will be derived from the architect's ceiling plans, so they in turn must be periodically checked
by overlay comparison with the latest reflected ceiling plans.

____ The consultants' plans must be overlay-compared with one another
as well as with the architectural ceiling plans. This process
assures that you'll find ceiling space interferences among the
building trades long before they become built-in sources of claims
for extras on the building site.

____ In addition to overlaying and comparing architectural, electrical,
plumbing, and HVAC, be sure to do overlay checks on structural
drawings. Although framing plans aren't necessarily produced by
the base sheet/overlay method, they should still be at the same
scale and position on drawing sheets as all other consultants' work.
It's the only way to facilitate this kind of checking and coordination. Although some structural engineers resist directives regarding their drawing scales and format, it's such a value to everyone
else on the job that such consistency should be written in as a requirement of their contract.

REFLECTED CEILING PLANS--INTRODUCTION Continued

ITEMS SUITED TO SYSTEMS DRAFTING, PASTE-UP, AND OVERLAY

____ As stated before, the reflected ceiling plans should be created as overlay sheets in direct reference to the floor plans. If no significant changes will occur on the floor plans, the reflected ceiling can be done directly on screened background sheets. But base/overlay drafting is your best bet for expediting plan changes that do occur and for maximizing coordination among all disciplines. When you use base and overlay separations, you won't have to redraw floor plan elements on the ceiling plan sheets every time changes are made. That can be a major time saver on most projects.

____ Reflected ceiling grids should be cut out of preprinted master grid sheets and assembled as paste-ups. A portion of grid can be drawn or computer plotted and copied in multiple at one-to-one size through contact printing on clear film. Then copies of the grid can be positioned, cut, and scotch taped into position on the background sheet or overlay (overlay is preferred) ceiling plan.

____ Combine screened images of the floor plans with solid-line images of the overlaid reflected ceiling plans when making progress prints and when making base sheets for the consulting engineers. That makes the architectural plan/ceiling plan work much clearer and more readable for the consultants' drafters. Just be careful that the screen used is coarse enough (at least 50%) so the screened lines are readable when overlay sheets are laid on them.

____ Use combined floor plan/ceiling plan sheets as base sheets for all ceiling work related to consultants' drafting. When printing the consultants' work, screen both the architectural floor plans and reflected ceiling plans so that only consultants' work appears in solid line. This further clarifies the drawings by visually distinctly separating the different kinds of construction information. Again, the screen should be coarse enough to guarantee readability.

____ Ceiling construction details are quite standard and should be a significant part of the office's master detail library.

____ Small unit appliques and tape drafting work well for handling the small symbols and special linework that's common to ceiling plans.

____ When larger elements are repeated on reflected ceiling plan overlays, such as repetitive room electrical layouts or ductwork, create the typical case, copy in multiple, and apply the copies as paste-ups on the overlays.

____ Reflected ceiling plans tend to require only a small number of notes which are repeated widely around the field of the drawing. That makes these drawings especially suitable for keynoting.

REFLECTED CEILING PLANS--CONSTRUCTION COMPONENTS

All items are assumed to require coordination checking with floor
plans; therefore those "coord checks" are not noted here. Also, all
electrical, communications, HVAC, plumbing, and vertical transporta-
tion are assumed to require cross checking with the architectural
ceiling plan as well as with one another. Especially important cases
are marked "mech" in the coordination check notes as an extra reminder.

Although structural coordination checking might also be taken for
granted and not listed, that is the most common area of oversight and
interference. Therefore, structural coordination checks are noted
where most important. Also included are reminders of another common
omission: provision for anchoring attached fixtures, furnishings, and
equipment with the ceiling structure. These are identified as "clg
anch."

IN   OK

___ ___   COLUMNS, POSTS, WALLS, AND CEILING-HIGH PARTITIONS
                ___ broken line or screened indication
            coord check: ___ struct ___ mech

___ ___   WALLS OR PARTITIONS EXTENDING THROUGH CEILING TO UNDERSIDE
            OF ROOF
                ___ solid-line indications ___ heights/elevation points
                ___ materials ___ dimensions/spacing ___ detail keys
                ___ notes/refs
            coord check: ___ struct ___ cross sect ___ mech

___ ___   EXPOSED CEILING BEAMS, GIRDERS, AND JOISTS
                ___ solid-line indications ___ heights/elevation points
                ___ materials ___ dimensions/spacing ___ detail keys
                ___ notes/refs
            coord check: ___ struct ___ cross sect ___ int elev
                ___ fin sched ___ mech

___ ___   SLOPE OF EXPOSED BEAMS
                ___ direction of slopes ___ low/high elevation points
            coord check: ___ struct ___ cross sect ___ int elev ___ mech

___ ___   CONCEALED BEAMS, GIRDERS, AND HEADERS
                ___ broken-line indications
                ___ materials ___ dimensions/spacing ___ detail keys
                    ___ notes/refs
            coord check: ___ struct ___ cross sect ___ mech

___ ___   SUSPENDED CEILING GRIDS 09100 (09120)
                ___ egg crates
                ___ light diffusers
                ___ dimensions/spacing ___ detail keys ___ notes/refs
            coord check: ___ struct ___ fin sched ___ mech ___ elec

REFLECTED CEILING PLANS--CONSTRUCTION COMPONENTS Continued

IN   OK

___ ___   INTEGRATED CEILINGS 13070 (13070)
          ___ dimensions/spacing ___ detail keys ___ notes/refs
          coord check: ___ struct ___ fin sched ___ mech ___ elec

___ ___   CEILING CONSTRUCTION AND FINISHES
          ___ WOOD PANELING 06400 (06420)
          ___ MIRRORS 08800 (08830)
          ___ SUSPENSION SYSTEM 09100 (09120)
          ___ ACOUSTICAL SUSPENSION SYSTEM 09100 (09130)
          ___ GYPSUM LATH AND PLASTER 09200 (09202)
          ___ METAL LATH AND PLASTER 09200 (09203)
          ___ GYPSUM WALLBOARD 09250 (09260 to 09280)
          ___ TILE 09300 (09310 to 09370)
          ___ ACOUSTICAL TILE 09500 (09512)
          ___ materials ___ dimensions ___ detail keys ___ notes/refs
          coord check: ___ struct ___ clg anch ___ fin sched

___ ___   SPECIAL CEILING TREATMENTS
          ___ WATERPROOFING IN WET ROOMS 07100 (07100)
          ___ DAMPPROOFING 07100 (07150)
          ___ THERMAL INSULATION 07200 (07200)
          ___ FIREPROOFING 07200 (07250)
          ___ ACOUSTICAL 09500 (09500 to 09513)
          ___ X-RAY AND RADIATION SHIELDING 13090 (13090)
          ___ ELECTROMAGNETIC SHIELDING 16600 (16650)
          ___ materials ___ dimensions ___ detail keys ___ notes/refs
          coord check: ___ code ___ specs ___ struct ___ fin sched

___ ___   SLOPE OF CEILINGS
          ___ direction of slopes ___ low/high elevation points
          coord check: ___ cross sect ___ int elev ___ mech

___ ___   CHANGES IN CEILING PLANE
          ___ dividing lines ___ heights/elevation points
          ___ materials ___ dimensions ___ detail keys ___ notes/refs
          coord check: ___ cross sect ___ int elev ___ mech

___ ___   FURRED CEILINGS AND SOFFITS
          ___ edge lines ___ heights/elevation points
          ___ materials ___ dimensions ___ detail keys ___ notes/refs
          coord check: ___ cross sect ___ int elev ___ mech

___ ___   ATTIC OR CEILING SPACE SEPARATORS
          ___ draft or fire stops
          ___ attic limit lines
          ___ broken-line indications
          ___ heights/elevation points
          ___ materials ___ dimensions ___ detail keys ___ notes/refs
          coord check: ___ code ___ struct ___ cross sect ___ mech

REFLECTED CEILING PLANS--CONSTRUCTION COMPONENTS   Continued

IN   OK

___ ___   EXPANSION JOINTS 05800 (05801)
          ___ materials ___ dimensions ___ detail keys ___ notes/refs
          coord check: ___ specs ___ struct ___ cross sect

___ ___   RECESSES
          ___ edge lines ___ heights/elevation points
          ___ materials ___ dimensions ___ detail keys ___ notes/refs
          coord check: ___ clg anch ___ fin sched ___ mech ___ elec

___ ___   COFFERS
          ___ edge lines ___ heights/elevation points
          ___ materials ___ dimensions ___ detail keys ___ notes/refs
          coord check: ___ clg anch ___ fin sched ___ mech ___ elec

___ ___   STAIRS
          ___ soffits under stairs and landings
          ___ soffits and furring at open stair ceiling penetration
          ___ materials ___ dimensions ___ detail keys ___ notes/refs
          coord check: ___ struct ___ stair sect ___ cross sect
          ___ int elev ___ fin sched

___ ___   THRU-CEILING ESCALATOR OPENINGS 14700 (14710)
          ___ soffits under escalators
          ___ soffits and furring at ceiling penetration
          ___ materials ___ dimensions ___ detail keys ___ notes/refs
          coord check: ___ struct ___ cross sect ___ int elev
          ___ fin sched ___ elec

___ ___   EXTERIOR OVERHANG SOFFIT REFLECTED PLANS
          ___ fascia line
          ___ louver or mesh soffit vents
          ___ trim
          ___ screeds
          ___ control joints
          ___ expansion joints
          ___ edge lines ___ heights/elevation points
          ___ materials ___ dimensions ___ detail keys ___ notes/refs
          coord check: ___ struct ___ ext elev ___ cross sect

___ ___   VALANCES 12500 (12503)
          ___ edge lines ___ heights/elevation points
          ___ materials ___ dimensions ___ detail keys ___ notes/refs
          coord check: ___ clg anch ___ cross sect ___ int elev
          ___ fin sched ___ mech ___ elec

___ ___   DRAPE OR BLIND CEILING TRACKS 12500 (12501 to 12527)
          ___ detail keys ___ notes/refs
          coord check: ___ clg anch ___ int elev ___ hardwr sched

REFLECTED CEILING PLANS--CONSTRUCTION COMPONENTS Continued

IN   OK

___ ___   SLIDING DOOR TRACKS
          ___ FIRE DOORS 08300 (08310)
          ___ GLASS DOORS 08300 (08370)
          ___ WOOD 08200 (08210)
          ___ detail keys ___ notes/refs
          coord check: ___ struct ___ clg anch ___ int elev
                        ___ door sched ___ hardwr sched

___ ___   FOLDING DOOR TRACKS 08300 (08350)
          ___ detail keys ___ notes/refs
          coord check: ___ struct ___ clg anch ___ int elev
                        ___ door sched ___ hardwr sched

___ ___   OVERHEAD DOOR SUPPORTS AND TRACKS 08300 (08331/08360)
          ___ detail keys ___ notes/refs
          coord check: ___ struct ___ clg anch ___ int elev
                        ___ door sched ___ hardwr sched

___ ___   DEMOUNTABLE PARTITIONS AND TRACKS 10600 (10610)
          ___ detail keys ___ notes/refs
          coord check: ___ struct ___ clg anch ___ int elev
                        ___ fin sched ___ hardwr sched

___ ___   MOVABLE PARTITIONS AND TRACKS 10600 (10615 to 10617)
          ___ detail keys ___ notes/refs
          coord check: ___ struct ___ clg anch ___ int elev
                        ___ fin sched ___ hardwr sched

___ ___   CEILING SUPPORTED TOILET AND SHOWER STALL PARTITIONS
          10150 (10160 to 10170)
          ___ detail keys ___ notes/refs
          coord check: ___ struct ___ clg anch ___ int elev

___ ___   HANGERS AND HOOKS 05500 (05507)
          ___ location dimensions ___ detail keys ___ notes/refs
          coord check: ___ struct ___ clg anch

___ ___   CEILING-MOUNTED CABINETS 06400 (06410)
          ___ materials ___ dimensions ___ detail keys ___ notes/refs
          coord check: ___ struct ___ clg anch ___ int elev

___ ___   CEILING-MOUNTED CASEWORK 12300 (12300)
          ___ materials ___ dimensions ___ detail keys ___ notes/refs
          coord check: ___ struct ___ clg anch ___ int elev

REFLECTED CEILING PLANS--CONSTRUCTION COMPONENTS   Continued

IN   OK

___ ___   WOOD BATTENS AND TRIM 06400 (06425)
           ___ dimensions/spacing ___ detail keys ___ notes/refs
           coord check: ___ int elev ___ fin sched

___ ___   NOISE BARRIERS IN SUSPENDED CEILING SPACES AT LOW PARTITION
           LINES 09500 (09530)
           ___ materials ___ detail keys ___ notes/refs
           coord check: ___ struct ___ clg anch ___ mech

___ ___   LIGHT FIXTURES 16500 (16501 to 16515)
           ___ surface mounted
           ___ recessed
           ___ lighting tracks
           ___ dimensions/spacing ___ detail keys ___ notes/refs
           coord check: ___ struct ___ clg anch ___ mech ___ elec

___ ___   CEILING-MOUNTED SPEAKERS 16700 (16770)
           ___ location dimensions where important ___ notes/refs
           coord check: ___ clg anch ___ elec

___ ___   ALARMS 16700 (16720)
           ___ location dimensions where important ___ notes/refs
           coord check: ___ clg anch ___ elec

___ ___   CEILING-MOUNTED CAMERAS AND MONITORS 16700 (16780)
           ___ location dimensions where important ___ notes/refs
           coord check: ___ clg anch ___ elec

___ ___   SMOKE AND HEAT DETECTORS 16700 (16725)
           ___ location dimensions where important ___ notes/refs
           coord check: ___ code ___ clg anch ___ elec

___ ___   MANUAL OR POWERED PROJECTION SCREENS 11130 (11131)
           ___ dimensions ___ notes/refs
           coord check: ___ struct ___ clg anch ___ int elev ___ elec

___ ___   FIRE SPRINKLER SYSTEM 15500 (15501 to 15510)
           (Integrated with suspended ceiling, lighting, and partitions.)
           ___ dimensions/spacing ___ detail keys ___ notes/refs
           coord check: ___ code ___ struct ___ clg anch ___ plumb
                ___ mech

___ ___   CATWALKS 05500 (05530)
           ___ materials ___ dimensions ___ detail keys ___ notes/refs
           coord check: ___ struct ___ clg anch ___ cross sect
                ___ int elev ___ mech

REFLECTED CEILING PLANS--CONSTRUCTION COMPONENTS Continued

IN   OK

___ ___   SERVICE LADDERS 05500 (05515)
             ___ materials ___ dimensions ___ detail keys ___ notes/refs
             coord check: ___ struct ___ clg anch ___ int elev ___ mech

___ ___   CEILING ACCESS PANELS 10220 (10220)
             ___ fold-down ladders
             ___ soffit scuttles
             ___ hinged or removable
             ___ materials ___ dimensions ___ detail keys ___ notes/refs
             coord check: ___ struct ___ clg anch ___ mech

___ ___   ROOF HATCHES 07800 (07830)
             ___ fusible link hatches
             ___ hinged or removable
             ___ materials ___ dimensions ___ detail keys ___ notes/refs
             coord check: ___ struct ___ roof ___ cross sect ___ mech

___ ___   THRU-CEILING SHAFTS
             ___ dimensions ___ detail keys ___ notes/refs
             coord check: ___ struct ___ cross sect ___ mech

___ ___   CHASES
             ___ dimensions ___ detail keys ___ notes/refs
             coord check: ___ struct ___ roof ___ cross sect ___ mech

___ ___   CHUTES
             ___ materials ___ dimensions ___ detail keys ___ notes/refs
             coord check: ___ struct ___ cross sect ___ mech

___ ___   FUTURE SHAFTS
             ___ dimensions ___ notes/refs
             coord check: ___ struct ___ cross sect ___ mech

___ ___   SKYLIGHTS 07800 (07810)
             ___ skylight sun screens
             ___ wire mesh skylight guards
             ___ fixed
             ___ operable
             ___ materials ___ dimensions ___ detail keys ___ notes/refs
             coord check: ___ struct ___ roof ___ cross sect

    ___   MONITORS/ROOF WINDOWS 08650 (08655)
             ___ fixed
             ___ operable
             ___ materials ___ dimensions ___ detail keys ___ notes/refs
             coord check: ___ struct ___ roof ___ cross sect

REFLECTED CEILING PLANS--CONSTRUCTION COMPONENTS Continued

IN   OK

___ ___   LIGHT WELLS
          ___ dimensions ___ detail keys ___ notes/refs
          coord check: ___ struct ___ roof ___ cross sect ___ mech

___ ___   INTEGRATED CEILING RADIANT HEATING SYSTEM 15700 (15745/15750)
          ___ dimensions/spacing ___ detail keys ___ notes/refs
          coord check: ___ fin sched ___ mech ___ elec

___ ___   LOUVERS 10200 (10200)
          ___ grilles
          ___ registers
          ___ materials ___ dimensions ___ detail keys ___ notes/refs
          coord check: ___ mech ___ clg anch

___ ___   AIR DISTRIBUTION 15800 (15800)
          ___ diffusers
          ___ return air vents
          ___ unit heaters
          ___ unit ventilators
          ___ fans
          ___ exhaust fans and flues
          ___ locations ___ detail keys ___ notes/refs
          coord check: ___ struct ___ clg anch ___ plumb ___ elec

___ ___   EXPOSED DUCTWORK 15800 (15840)
          ___ locations ___ detail keys ___ notes/refs
          coord check: ___ struct ___ clg anch ___ plumb ___ elec

___ ___   NOISE- AND VIBRATION-DAMPENING CONNECTORS FOR FAN MOTORS AND
          OTHER NOISY, CEILING-MOUNTED EQUIPMENT 15200 (15200)
          ___ detail keys ___ notes/refs
          coord check: ___ clg anch ___ mech ___ elec

___ ___   HOISTS AND CRANES 14300 (14300)
          ___ location dimensions ___ detail keys ___ notes/refs
          coord check: ___ struct ___ clg anch ___ cross sect
               ___ int elev ___ mech ___ elec

CHAPTER EIGHT--SCHEDULES   8.0 - 8.3

SCHEDULES--DOOR SCHEDULES

IN   OK

___ ___ DOOR TYPES DRAWN IN ELEVATION (1/2" scale is typical.)

___ ___ SYMBOL AND IDENTIFYING NUMBER AT EACH DOOR

___ ___ DOOR SIZES: ___ WIDTHS ___ HEIGHTS ___ THICKNESSES

___ ___ DOOR TYPES: ___ MATERIALS ___ FINISHES
         (The number of doors of each type and size is sometimes noted.)

___ ___ OPERATING TYPE: ___ SLIDING ___ SINGLE-ACTING
         ___ DOUBLE-ACTING ___ DUTCH ___ PIVOT ___ 2-HINGE
         ___ 3-HINGE

___ ___ KICKPLATES

___ ___ FIRE RATING IF REQUIRED

___ ___ LOUVERS ___ UNDERCUTS FOR VENTILATION

___ ___ SCREENS

___ ___ MEETING STILES

___ ___ DOOR GLAZING ___ TRANSOMS ___ BORROWED LIGHTS

___ ___ DETAIL KEY REFERENCE SYMBOLS: ___ SILLS ___ JAMBS
         ___ HEADERS

___ ___ MANUFACTURERS ___ CATALOG NUMBERS
         (If not covered in Specifications.)

___ ___ METAL FRAMES: ___ ELEVATIONS ___ SCHEDULE ___ DETAILS

SCHEDULES--WINDOW SCHEDULES

IN   OK

___ ___   WINDOW TYPES DRAWN IN ELEVATION
           (1/2" scale is typical.)

___ ___   WINDOW SYMBOL AND IDENTIFYING NUMBER AT EACH DRAWING

___ ___   WINDOW SIZE ___ WIDTH ___ HEIGHT

___ ___   WINDOW TYPE ___ DIRECTION OF MOVEMENT OF OPERABLE SASH AS
           SEEN FROM EXTERIOR
           (Number of windows of each type and size is sometimes noted.)

___ ___   GLASS THICKNESS AND TYPE

___ ___   NOTE: FIXED ___ OBSCURE ___ WIRE ___ TEMPERED
           ___ DOUBLE GLAZING ___ TINTED

___ ___   SCREENS

___ ___   DETAIL KEY REFERENCE SYMBOLS: ___ SILLS ___ JAMBS
           ___ HEADERS

___ ___   MANUFACTURERS ___ CATALOG NUMBERS
           (If not covered in Specifications.)

___ ___   METAL FRAME STOREFRONT OR CURTAIN WALL SYSTEM: ___ ELEVATIONS
           ___ SCHEDULE ___ DETAILS

SCHEDULES--FINISH SCHEDULES

IN   OK

___ ___   ROOM NAME AND/OR IDENTIFYING NUMBER

___ ___   FLOOR: THICKNESS ___ MATERIAL ___ FINISH

___ ___   BASE: HEIGHT ___ MATERIAL ___ FINISH

___ ___   WALLS: MATERIALS ___ FINISHES
          (Walls may be identified by compass direction code symbol if
          finishes vary from wall to wall. Note waterproofing and
          waterproof membrane wall construction.)

___ ___   WAINSCOT: HEIGHT ___ MATERIAL ___ FINISH

___ ___   CEILING: MATERIAL ___ FINISH

___ ___   SOFFITS: MATERIAL ___ FINISH

___ ___   CABINETS: MATERIAL SPECIES AND GRADE ___ FINISH

___ ___   SHELVING: MATERIAL ___ FINISH

___ ___   DOORS: MATERIAL ___ FINISH
          (If not covered in Door Schedule.)

___ ___   TRIM AND MILLWORK: MATERIAL SPECIES AND GRADE ___ FINISH

___ ___   MISCELLANEOUS REMARKS OR NOTES

___ ___   COLORS: STAIN AND PAINT ___ MANUFACTURER AND TRADE NAMES OR
          NUMBERS
          (If not covered in Specifications. Sometimes left for later
          decision with provision for paint allowance by bidders.)

___ ___   EXTERIOR FINISHES: ___ EXTERIOR WALLS ___ SILLS ___ TRIM
          ___ POSTS ___ GUTTERS AND LEADERS ___ FLASHING AND VENTS
          ___ FASCIAS ___ RAILINGS ___ DECKING ___ SOFFITS
          (Included in Finish Schedule if not covered in Specifications.)

9.0

CHAPTER NINE--EXTERIOR WALL SECTIONS   9.0   - 9.5

EXTERIOR WALL SECTIONS

Exterior wall sections are primarily to show the detail bubble key
references of major junctures in construction: floor slab and foundation wall, sills, headers, spandrels, upper floor slab at the exterior
wall, ceiling at. the exterior wall, roof construction at the exterior
wall, and roof parapets and/or overhangs.

As a key map to more specific detail construction drawings, wall sections serve much the same function as building cross sections. They
are a map for finding other drawings and not necessarily definitive
construction drawings in themselves.

Wall section information is often adequately covered by building cross
section drawings. Thus even though wall sections may have been created
as part of the design process, it may be redundant to include them
as a part of working drawings. If they are included, then the detail
reference key bubbles should not be repeated on the overall cross
sections and the larger scale wall sections.

Because of the schematic and referral nature of this type of drawing,
this list does not include "coord check" notes or the CSI-coordinated
reference numbers. Consider this list just a reminder of basic components of wall section key drawings.   You will cover all coordination checks and CSI number coordinations through the other chapters
in this checklist manual.

IN   OK

____ ____   EXISTING AND NEW FINISH GRADE LINES WITH ELEVATIONS

____ ____   FOOTINGS AND FOUNDATION WALLS
            ___ materials ___ dimensions ___ detail keys ___ notes/refs

____ ____   DRAINS
            ___ drain tiles
            ___ crushed rock drain tile bed
            ___ roof drain connections to storm sewer
            ___ materials ___ dimensions ___ detail keys ___ notes/refs

____ ____   BASEMENT AREAWAY
            ___ areaway wall and footing
            ___ drain
            ___ window or hatch section
            ___ materials ___ dimensions ___ detail keys ___ notes/refs

____ ____   BASEMENT WALL MEMBRANE WATERPROOFING
            ___ materials ___ height ___ detail keys ___ notes/refs

EXTERIOR WALL SECTIONS Continued

IN   OK

___ ___ PIPE AND SLEEVES THAT PENETRATE WATERPROOFING
         ___ heights/sizes ___ detail keys ___ notes/refs

___ ___ BASEMENT OR FOUNDATION WALL GIRDER RECESSES
         ___ heights/sizes ___ detail keys ___ notes/refs

___ ___ ADJACENT PAVING AND WALKWAYS
         ___ slope away from building
         ___ slope to drain
         ___ materials ___ dimensions ___ detail keys ___ notes/refs

___ ___ ADJACENT STOOPS
         ___ landings
         ___ paving
         ___ materials ___ dimensions ___ detail keys ___ notes/refs

___ ___ EXTERIOR SLAB FOOTINGS OR FROST CURBS
         ___ tamped fill
         ___ sand and gravel fill
         ___ vapor barrier
         ___ reinforcing
         ___ materials ___ dimensions ___ detail keys ___ notes/refs

___ ___ DOWELS CONNECTING SLABS TO FOOTINGS OR FOUNDATION WALLS
         ___ locations ___ detail keys ___ notes/refs

___ ___ MASONRY WALLS
         ___ types (See Floor Plans)
         ___ air space and weep holes
         ___ courses and header courses
         ___ sill flashing
         ___ head flashing
         ___ anchors and reinforcing
         ___ grouting
         ___ parging
         ___ caulking
         ___ materials ___ dimensions ___ detail keys ___ notes/refs

___ ___ CURTAIN WALLS
         ___ types (See Floor Plans)
         ___ support angles
         ___ anchors
         ___ weep holes
         ___ movement joints
         ___ caulking
         ___ sealants
         ___ materials ___ dimensions ___ detail keys ___ notes/refs

EXTERIOR WALL SECTIONS Continued

IN   OK

___ ___ WOOD FRAME WALLS
         ___ mudsill
         ___ blocking
         ___ floor joists
         ___ subfloor
         ___ plates
         ___ studs
         ___ sills
         ___ headers
         ___ double top plates
         ___ blocking
         ___ ceiling/roof joists
         ___ rafters
         ___ purlins
         ___ girts
         ___ dimensions ___ detail keys ___ notes/refs

___ ___ GIRDERS, BEAMS, AND JOISTS
         ___ hangers
         ___ anchors
         ___ sills
         ___ stirrups
         ___ pockets
         ___ ledgers
         ___ bearing plates
         ___ bridging and blocking
         ___ materials ___ dimensions ___ detail keys ___ notes/refs

___ ___ FLOOR CONSTRUCTION
         ___ connection at wall
         ___ subflooring
         ___ floor slabs and metal deck
         ___ topping
         ___ finish topping
         ___ materials ___ dimensions ___ detail keys ___ notes/refs

___ ___ WATERPROOFING AT WET ROOMS
         ___ materials ___ height ___ detail keys ___ notes/refs

___ ___ LINTELS
         ___ headers
         ___ masonry ledges
         ___ steel wall angles
         ___ spandrel beams
         ___ spandrel angles
         ___ materials ___ height/sizes ___ detail keys ___ notes/refs

EXTERIOR WALL SECTIONS Continued

IN   OK

____ ____ DOORS AND WINDOWS
           ____ sills and saddles
           ____ head framing
           ____ caulking
           ____ flashing
           ____ trim
           ____ stools and aprons
           ____ anchors to wall
           ____ materials ____ dimensions ____ detail keys ____ notes/refs

____ ____ LIGHT COVES
           ____ coffers
           ____ valances
           ____ materials ____ dimensions ____ detail keys ____ notes/refs

____ ____ WALL AND CEILING COMPONENTS
           ____ rigid or batt terminal insulation
           ____ fireproof construction
           ____ soundproofing
           ____ acoustical treatments
           ____ wainscots
           ____ finishes
           ____ materials ____ dimensions ____ detail keys ____ notes/refs

____ ____ SUSPENDED CEILINGS
           ____ connection at wall
           ____ partial view of tees and hangers
           ____ materials ____ dimensions ____ detail keys ____ notes/refs

____ ____ MASONRY WALL TOP PLATE OR LEDGERS
           ____ plate anchors
           ____ beam pockets
           ____ materials ____ dimensions ____ detail keys ____ notes/refs

____ ____ PARAPET WATERPROOFING
           ____ flashing reglet
           ____ flashing and counterflashing
           ____ overflows
           ____ materials ____ dimensions ____ detail keys ____ notes/refs

____ ____ PARAPET CAP
           ____ wash toward roof
           ____ parapet expansion and construction joints
           ____ materials ____ dimensions ____ detail keys ____ notes/refs

EXTERIOR WALL SECTIONS Continued

IN   OK

____ ____ EDGE FLASHING
           ____ gutter and gutter connectors
           ____ gravel stop
           ____ cap flashing
           ____ cant strips
           ____ eave snow guards
           ____ materials ___ dimensions ___ detail keys ___ notes/refs

____ ____ TRUSSES
           ____ connection at wall
           ____ materials ___ dimensions ___ detail keys ___ notes/refs

____ ____ OVERHANG
           ____ fascia
           ____ soffit
           ____ soffit vents
           ____ trim
           ____ expansion joints
           ____ materials ___ dimensions ___ detail keys ___ notes/refs

____ ____ ROOF DECKING OR SHEATHING
           ____ cant and flashing at roof edge or parapet
           ____ railings
           ____ materials ___ dimensions ___ detail keys ___ notes/refs